THE OUTDOOR Family Fun Guide

A Complete Camping, Hiking, Canoeing, Nature Watching, Mountain Biking, Skiing, and General Fun Book for Parents and Kids

Michael Hodgson (Gear Carrier, Dad)
and Nicole Hodgson (Trail Boss, Daughter)

RAGGED MOUNTAIN PRESS • CAMDEN, MAINE

NEW YORK • SAN FRANCISCO • WASHINGTON, D.C.
AUCKLAND • BOGOTÁ • CARACAS • LISBON • LONDON
MADRID • MEXICO CITY • MILAN • MONTREAL • NEW DELHI
SAN JUAN • SINGAPORE • SYDNEY • TOKYO • TORONTO

International Marine/
Ragged Mountain Press
A Division of The **McGraw-Hill** *Companies*

10 9 8 7 6 5 4 3 2 1

Library of Congress Cataloging-in-Publication Data

Hodgson, Michael.
The outdoor family fun guide : a complete camping, hiking, canoeing, nature watching, mountain biking, skiing, and general fun book for parents and kids / Michael Hodgson and Nicole Hodgson.
p. cm.
ISBN 0-07-029184-5
1. Outdoor recreation—United States. 2. Outdoor recreation—United States—Planning. 3. Family recreation—United States. 4. Family recreation—United States—Planning. I. Hodgson, Nicole. II. Title.
GV191.4H63 1998
796—dc21 98-9822
CIP

Questions regarding the content of this book should be addressed to:

Ragged Mountain Press
P.O. Box 220
Camden, ME 04843
www.raggedmountainpress.com

Questions regarding the ordering of this book should be addressed to:

The McGraw-Hill Companies
Customer Service Department
P.O. Box 547
Blacklick, OH 43004
Retail customers: 1-800-262-4729
Bookstores: 1-800-233-4726

The Outdoor Family Fun Guide is printed on 60-pound Renew Opaque Vellum, an acid-free paper which contains 50 percent recycled waste paper (preconsumer) and 10 percent postconsumer waste paper.

Printed by R.R. Donnelley, Crawfordsville, IN
Design by Ann Aspell
Production by PD & PS Sagamore Beach, MA
Project management by Janet Robbins
Edited by John Vigor, Tom McCarthy
Photo on page 7 by David J. Mac Donald; photo on page 30 courtesy Adventure Medical Kits; photo on page 111 by Mark Lord; all other photos by the author

For Nicole. Through your eyes I am constantly reminded to see the world for what it is, a place full of inspiration and wonder.

For Therese, my partner in life.

Contents

Introduction

PERHAPS IT IS A NATURAL CURIOSITY ABOUT THINGS FURRY, fuzzy, and new. Perhaps it is the desire to discover wide-open spaces, to frolic, tumble, and hide; or perhaps it is the pull of an unknown spirit. Whatever it is, nature and children go together like peanut butter and jelly.

Take one look at the wide-eyed expression of a little girl who has just blown with all her might on a milkweed and can hardly believe the white fluffy explosion that she has caused, and you start to understand the need for sharing the outdoors with children. The outdoors urges discovery and learning—it doesn't allow for less. Nature and the outdoors provide for personal inspiration like nothing else can. Every minute becomes an individual expression of wonder, delight, and enlightenment.

You don't have to be a disciple of John Muir or Henry David Thoreau to pass along to your children the joys of being outdoors. You need only patience, wonder, and a sense of fun to share the outdoors; but nature is the grand instructor, so expect to learn as much about it from your children as they do from you.

"But children are difficult to teach."

"They're too young to appreciate camping."

"They will never enjoy being out away from the television for more than one night."

"They'll get too tired."

"They . . ."

I have heard it all.

We are growing up in an age dominated by computers, the Internet, television, fast cars, and a faster lifestyle. Parents seem to find more and more excuses for not giving their children the experience of the wilderness. They don't seem to have the patience to try. But believe me, taking your kids hiking or camping doesn't take much effort, as long as you keep one rule in mind: "See everything through a child's eyes."

Children want to be involved, even the youngest ones, with planning, packing, carrying, and guiding. It becomes very obvious to them when they are considered extra baggage, just "in the way." If you want your children to learn about the outdoors, to enjoy every minute in the sun, then the learning must start at home.

It is true that if you take kids along, you will not be able to camp as freely as you once did; you can no longer just pick up at a moment's notice, hike for miles, and gaze silently at nothing in particular for hours. On the other hand, you could never have camped as you now have the opportunity to do, seeing everything through the inquisitive, yearning, searching, and undeniably joyful eyes of your child.

You will understand soon, if you do not already, that experiencing nature in the uninhibited manner of children is by far the best way. It doesn't matter how far or how much, how high or how difficult, just as long as there is discovery and fun along the way. Prepare your parental ego for the shock that perhaps your child will be more interested in running around a meadow chasing butterflies than in climbing an "incredible" peak. Then, instead of fretting, you will be able to join in your child's simple joy.

When I look back upon my days as a youngster, I remember most vividly moments spent wandering in the mountains of western Canada and northern Colorado with my mother and father. We never went camping (I went to summer camp for that), but every Sunday was mine for hiking and exploring, mine to feed the chipmunks with my mother or to scramble through rock fields with my father. My parents were wonderful in not dictating their needs to me. Instead, they allowed my inquisitiveness to lead us all on.

It is with that same outlook that I now share the wilds with my own daughter, Nicole, aged 15. When she was younger she took great pride in "helping" Daddy up the steep hills, and in deciding when to have a snack, or where to explore next. Now, I take great pride in simply trying to keep up with her strength and purpose. Through Nicole, my own sense of discovery and joy for the outdoors is heightened.

She began camping when she was one month old. From those early moments beside a campfire under glittering stars, Nicole's love of the outdoors has grown steadily. Every family and every situation is unique, so not all parents are going to take their children camping or paddling or climbing, and certainly not at one month. It's worth considering, though, that the outdoors offers each and every child a special opportunity. I encourage parents and children to use and learn everything the wilderness has to offer. Bask in the simplicity, the wonder, the enlightenment, the sheer joy of being one with the world. I do not think you or your children will be disappointed.

CHAPTER 1

Gentle Beginnings

THERE MUST BE A BEGINNING, A KIND OF STARTING POINT TO everything. So it is in sharing the outdoors with children. But the first shared experiences often dictate whether or not your children will inherit your love of the outdoors. Starting with a grandiose idea to climb a favorite peak that the children have never seen before, or to camp in a remote and secluded spot that you remember as special, is a recipe for trouble.

I started taking Nicole camping before she was one year old, and I planned short excursions. Nikki, as she was then before she became a young woman, stayed close to home, in warm valleys with nearby meadows for crawling and simple exploring.

Keeping it simple (and remembering that this is all new to a child) is key to success in this adventure. Children do not need the high peaks, the spectacular views, the raging rapids. Think about it. You probably didn't start that way either.

Children will find joy in clouds, flowers, crawfish hunting, splashing, rolling down a grassy knoll, watching a multicolored bug, or playing one of a hundred different nature-discovery games with you. It is not fun to be cold, sunburned, hungry, thirsty, exhausted, or frustrated. Make your first outings fun for the children and you will discover your excitement and adventure through their eyes.

The question I am most often asked is: "When is a child old enough to begin hiking and camping?" Quite frankly, that depends on your child; there are no hard-and-fast rules. Some generally acknowledged guidelines should be considered, however. The following guide will help you to decide where and when to begin, but remember that the only firm guide is each child's particular personality and physical condition. Whatever the activity, you must let them pace themselves.

INFANTS

Pediatricians recommend that parents wait until the child is 5 months old before venturing out into the wilderness. At this age, infants can easily sit up and support their own weight. They will also have fallen into a fairly regular sleep pattern. Use a sturdy child carrier that is both safe and secure for the child and also comfortable for you.

TODDLERS

Between the ages of 2 and 4 years, children are still getting used to the idea of balancing on two points instead of four. Short hikes, from half a mile to 2 miles, are ideal as long as the terrain is flat and secure to walk on. You can assess your child's attention span by taking regular walks in a neighborhood park. Expect a focused attention of around 10 minutes for the young child and up to 30 minutes for older children.

AGES 5 TO 9 YEARS

Longer hikes at a slow pace over easy terrain are now possible. Children are beginning to develop more stamina and concen-

The wilderness is no place for competition. Set your own pace and don't worry about what someone else is doing.

Before turning in for the night, nibble on some high-calorie food. The fuel your body now has to burn will help it stay warmer during the night.

Leave only footprints. Take only memories. 

tration. This is an ideal age to start getting your child involved in most aspects of the trip, from planning and packing to helping lead the party. The older your child is in this age group, the better they will respond to moderate goals. Once again, these must be shared goals, not unrealistic attempts on the parents' part to "motivate" the child up an impossible hill or along a 10-mile "death march."

AGES 10 TO 13 YEARS

Children are in better physical condition by now, and emotionally they are more able to handle moderately challenging situations. But they are also more likely to question the worth of anything extremely difficult. Hikes of up to 10 miles are possible. Children in this age group thrive on being leaders; diplomatic and judicious support from parents is key. Menu planning, route finding, cooking, and setting up camp are reasonable tasks for children of this age, but be careful that they do not take on too much or they will begin to feel as if all they ever do is work.

AGES 14 TO 18 YEARS

In this age group, trips of 12 miles become reasonable. Personally, though, I prefer to hike no more than 8 miles. Members of this age group can take more responsibility for choosing the terrain to hike through, and for setting goals. But the rule remains the same: All choices must be a group decision, or the children might feel they are simply being "dragged along."

Remember that children are encountering growth spurts during this period and are vulnerable to stress and overuse injuries. Use caution and listen to your children. Don't let them suffer pain. They may need to take a break or cut short a hike.

Guidelines and rules aside, the choice of what to do rests with you and your family. No two personalities, no two children, are the same. What may work for my family may not work for yours. Flexibility and adaptability need to be added to your growing arsenal of outdoor camping techniques.

No matter how old your children, or how experienced you personally may be in the outdoors, if any of your family has never set foot in the wilderness you would be wise to proceed slowly. The foundation for a love of outdoor adventuring must be laid carefully. Plan some simple day trips to local parks and wilderness preserves. Just walking, skiing, biking, or wandering outdoors, drinking from a canteen, carrying a day pack, wearing hiking or ski boots, or eating trail food, will be novelty enough for your family.

With a little flexibility even a 5-month-old child can start her outdoor adventuring.

Blend in with the environment at all times.
Save rowdy games for other places.

On your first day trip you will have much to do and consider. Do your family members have the right clothes? Do their shoes and packs fit? Did everyone bring plenty of water? How about snacks and a trail lunch? Does everyone have rain gear? Who is carrying the first-aid kit? Who knows how to use it? Is the trip well suited to all the participants? How is the walking, skiing, or biking pace?

Even though you must assume leadership because of your experience, it is important to remember that this is supposed to be fun and relaxing. So, relax and enjoy yourself. Involve everyone in the process. Don't be the only one running around frantically trying to make sure everything is getting done. Assign responsibilities. Put someone in charge of the first-aid kit. Designate a cook, even though this will be a sack lunch, to plan and pack the meal. Get everyone involved in checking gear and making sure the day packs are equally loaded, so no one carries too much or too little.

Above all, listen to your family. Set the pace of the hike to suit the slowest and weakest (not necessarily the youngest) member of your hiking team. This is not to embarrass that member but simply to ensure that the pace will not overtire anybody. When selecting this member, diplomacy is crucial. Fellow playmates will be quick to abuse and tease a "weakling." Whatever reason you give, pick a positive one.

Choosing a destination is perhaps the hardest task of all. Everyone has a favorite memory, a most spectacular view, a most unbelievable campsite. The trouble is, what is absolutely breathtaking to you may not seem to someone else to be worth the effort of reaching. This is especially true with chil-

See animals and plants for what they are—more than a scientific name in an identification book.

Plan your trips well within the abilities of all—adults and children.

dren. Parents quickly learn that fantastic views are not enough to stimulate children into "oohs" and "aahs." Children seem to prefer doing to looking. They like lakes to splash in, streams to wade through, meadows to romp around, trees to climb up, hills to roll down, easy rocks to scramble on, mud for pies, and someone to play with.

Keeping seasons in mind, I have been able to plan fairly exciting outings for my daughter and me. As a young child, Nikki loved colors, smelling wildflowers, watching insects, skipping rocks on a smooth lake surface, discovering cloud shapes, and rolling down hills with reckless abandon. A trail covered with fall leaves to kick and bound through was an additional enticement. Find out what turns your child on and then go for it—plan your trip around his or her sensory pleasures.

Be prepared to get down and dirty with your children; experiencing the outdoors with them means participating, not just watching. Perhaps one of my most vivid memories when I was teaching outdoor education is of a young boy who found it distasteful to get dirty. We were gathered around a campfire enjoying gooey s'mores (chocolate bars, toasted marshmallows, and graham crackers mashed together into a wonderfully messy and delicious sandwich). I happened to glance away from the campfire and noticed a neatly dressed boy standing by himself. Wondering what was wrong, since everyone else was laughing so hard, I went over to him and encouraged him to join us around the fire.

"Naw," he replied, "Can't hang with that stuff—too messy you know."

Too bad! Because of his attitude and upbringing (I've still never seen a limo shinier than the one that came to pick him up the next morning) he was unable to fully enjoy the evening with his friends.

This is not to say that you have to get filthy to appreciate the outdoors. But a little dirt should not hold you back as parents or children. When I worked at a summer camp as the trip director and nature instructor, one of the favorite classes was Swamp Mucking. Wading waist-deep through a prepared route into the swamp to view wildlife at eye level brought squeals of delight, even from refined 16-year-olds. Interestingly, I had several letters from parents, having heard about the class through their children's letters, wanting to join in. So go for it with your children; you'll never find a better excuse to let your hair down and have fun.

With a child along, it's not how far and how fast but rather how interesting.

Be careful to replace all gear in your pack—the most gear is lost, or litter left behind, at the place where you stop to rest.

Always camp out of sight of others and the trail.

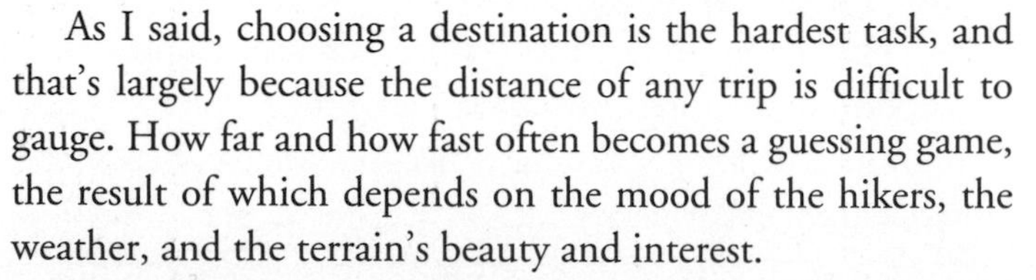

As I said, choosing a destination is the hardest task, and that's largely because the distance of any trip is difficult to gauge. How far and how fast often becomes a guessing game, the result of which depends on the mood of the hikers, the weather, and the terrain's beauty and interest.

How do you control this aspect of a hike? Well, you really can't do much about the mood of the hikers, short of keeping an excellent sense of humor. Neither can you do much about the weather, except to be prepared for anything with the appropriate clothing and gear. But you can plan and control the difficulty and interest of the terrain you will be traveling through.

Plan easy hikes, especially for the members of your group who might suspect this is not really going to be fun. I would recommend a hike of less than five miles under most circumstances, and a rise and fall in elevation of no more than 500 feet. To ensure that everyone will have a wonderful time, the hike itself (not just the destination) must be memorable. Ad-

Replace all the standard split-rings on your pack with sturdier ones from a hardware store.

Try to blend—neon colors belong in Las Vegas, not in the woods.

mittedly, huffing, puffing, and wheezing is memorable, but it's not the kind of memory most children seek. Take frequent rest breaks, eat plenty of snacks, splash through a stream or two, play entertaining games—do anything to have fun.

Pay close attention to your family because their eyes and the tones of their voices are full of valuable information. Are they looking around and eager, or are they looking at their feet? Are they feeling sore or overly tired? Is getting to the destination becoming more of a burden than a goal? It is acceptable to turn around at any time, particularly if the hike is just as important as the destination. How you turn around though, will determine whether this hike will be a success. Never make children (or adults for that matter) feel guilty about being responsible for an aborted trip. Never try to motivate an exhausted member of your group by cajoling or needling. Make the decision to turn around *your* idea, because you are feeling tired, or for any other reason that doesn't sound condescending or ridiculous.

If the reason is acceptable, no one will regret a decision to turn around or shorten a trip. The mountain or lake will always be there for another try. But your family and children may not be persuaded to go again if the last outing was so miserable that they never want to return. Most of the horror stories I have heard revolve around someone dragging them up over peaks and down through deep valleys, through pouring rain or worse. The whole idea for sharing the outdoors with our children is to have fun and expose them to a wonderful world full of discoveries.

Tips in a Nutshell

1. Plan your destination to be attractive and fun for all. Keep the hike fairly short, no longer than 5 miles. Keep the elevation gain and loss to a minimum—500 feet is about right. Appealing scenery, and interesting things to do and see, will spice up any hike. Keep your trip within the physical and emotional capabilities of everyone involved.
2. Favorite and nutritional snacks in addition to a tasty lunch are a must. Fruit, cheese sticks, and crackers are good for snacks. Include also good old raisins and peanuts (Gorp) mixed with M&Ms and other tidbits. Fruit juice in a box is fun but be sure to buy the real fruit juice, not the fruit-flavored mix. Pack carefully. Grapes and candy bars spread all over the inside of a pack aren't very appetizing.
3. Carry the bare-minimum. Make everything count—extra weight is not worth the extra pain. Children want to participate, and should, even the younger ones. My daughter, Nicole, was carrying a small pack when she was just 3 years old. All she carried was a small teddy bear and a box of juice, but it was important that she feel involved, and for her the teddy bear and juice were essential anyway. Don't pack canned goods, or two different items when one might do the job of both, or anything not necessary for your safety and comfort.
4. Everyone should carry some sort of signaling device. I carry a signal mirror and whistle. I would recommend that every member in a hiking party, not just the children, carry a whistle and know how and when to use it. Teach your children never to whistle unless they are in trouble. Also, teach them that signals in threes (three sharp and distinct blows on the whistle) indicate someone is in trouble.
5. Be prepared to get down and dirty with your children. Experience the outdoors with them, not just watching them.
6. Always have an emergency plan. You never know when a real

need or emergency will arise so it is best always to be prepared. Know where the nearest emergency room is. Involve your children in every emergency plan you make. They are never too young to hear how to take care of themselves. I have found that it is a good idea not only to let someone responsible know where you are going at all times, but also to be sure that you take along with you someone responsible, like another adult, just in case. Learn basic first aid and cardiopulmonary resuscitation (CPR) at the very least. It feels helpless to be in an emergency and not know what to do. The Red Cross gives instruction in first aid. No matter what, put safety first.

7. Children's skin is very sensitive, so use good sunblock. A hat and sunglasses are also very important as protection from the sun and heat. Protection from insects is important, too. Since insect repellent is such a noxious substance, however, I prefer shirts with long sleeves and long pants whenever possible. If insect repellent becomes absolutely necessary, apply it very sparingly and always keep it away from the eyes and mouth. Insect repellent in the eyes is painful at the very least, and sometimes becomes a medical emergency.
8. Children want and need their peers. I would encourage you to bring a close family playmate along for your children. Sharing with a friend makes things more enjoyable for them, and—believe it or not—will usually make the hike easier for you. You will have less entertaining to do.
9. Cultivate patience and a sense of humor. Without them, your efforts to share the outdoors with your children will be seriously hampered. Laughter, fun and games, silly pranks, and unexpected occurrences are part of being outdoors with children. Go with the flow and enjoy every moment together. If you can learn to laugh when a child covered with mud arrives for a ride home in the family car, you are ready to proceed as an outdoor leader. Good luck!

CHAPTER 2

The Equipment You Need

BEFORE HEADING OUT ON ANY CAMPING ADVENTURE, YOUR family must be properly equipped. This may be harder than it sounds, because there are many alternatives and choices, but you can make it easier by following some basic guidelines.

First, find out what equipment is available. Talk to friends about what they prefer and where they like to shop. Consult magazines that evaluate gear, such as *Backpacker, Canoe & Kayak,* or *Outside.* Talk to salespeople at your local outdoor store about your needs.

When you have enough information the choices will narrow, and you should be able to make fairly educated purchasing or borrowing decisions. Many outdoor specialty stores rent sleeping bags, tents, backpacks, stoves, and even child carriers. Some also rent boots; I would discourage this, however, because footwear is very individual. A rented boot could spell misery and a ruined trip.

General Outdoor Gear

Before you read the following list, it's important for you to realize that advice about outdoor gear can become dated within a year, sometimes sooner. I have done my best to ensure that all the advice given here is current and will not soon be outdated. I would recommend, however, if you have access to the Internet, that you log onto my website (http://www.adventurenetwork.com) for the most up-to-date advice.

THE BEST TENT

Choosing a tent can be a difficult task. If you go camping only with your children, then the decision becomes easier, but if you like to camp without the kids, then you must decide between buying two tents of the right size, and buying one that will sometimes be too small and sometimes too large.

I solved this dilemma by buying a relatively roomy two-person tent that we used under slightly cramped conditions until Nicole turned four. I then added a large nylon tarpaulin, which doesn't add much weight to my backpack. The tarp provided an "extra room" under which I was protected even in the worst rain, while my wife and daughter slept in the tent. The tarp also gave an extra benefit—it was something to sit and cook under in bad weather.

When Nicole was eight years old, and bringing a friend along for the fun, I opted for a second, lightweight two-person tent. Nicole and company slept under one roof and my wife and I under the other—sometimes several hundred yards apart, depending on how brave Nicole was feeling that evening. Now that my daughter is 15, we're back to a two-person tent when just the two of us head out on adventures. When we're thinking very lightweight, and have no fear of mosquitoes, we even do without a tent and simply take a tarp.

When you're buying a tent, buy quality. Blown stitches,

A sticky equipment zipper means trouble's brewing. Lubricate the slider and teeth with silicone or wax.

"waterproof" coatings that leak like a sieve, broken cheap fiberglass poles, and torn fabric are all candidates for the Nightmare Weekend Hall of Fame. Be sure the tent is roomy enough so you don't feel imprisoned, but not so roomy that you need porters to carry it. My tent and tarp have a combined weight of nine pounds.

The tent should have a generous rainfly that will provide adequate protection against the worst storm and still allow for ventilation and evaporation of condensation. The fabric of the tent body and rainfly should be tight when erected, with no obvious major sags or baggy material to flap and tear in the wind. Also, the rainfly should not touch the tent body since this may cause leaks and condensation.

Even the best tent will deteriorate if you don't care for it properly. Never store it damp for long periods because it will mildew and be ruined. Don't wear boots in the tent because abrasive sand or dirt can wear a hole in the floor. Periodically clean dirt and grime off the tent with a sponge, warm water, and mild soap. Never light a stove or lantern in a tent. You not only run the risk of melting fabric and destroying the tent, but it can lead to asphyxiation. Don't forget to seal the tent's seams—ask the salesperson to show you how.

SLEEPING BAG

When you're choosing a sleeping bag, the crucial question becomes synthetic-fill or down-fill. Down is more efficient in terms of a weight-to-warmth ratio, and more compact, but only synthetic fills, such as PolarGuard, Lite Loft, Hollofil, or Quallofil, will maintain their loft (fluffiness) and warmth even when wet. Down turns into a heavy, soggy, cold mess. I would recommend synthetic fill for children at all times. I use a down sleeping bag because it is light, but I am very careful to keep it protected from the elements, even to the point of storing it in a waterproof stuffsack.

Better camping gear does not make a better camper. You cannot buy experience.

Mummy-shaped bags are more efficient at keeping the body warm than are other shapes, but some people find them too constricting. Ask the salesperson to lay out the bags you are looking at so that you can climb in them. If you are buying bags to zip together, make sure that the zippers are compatible and that you purchase right- and left-zipper bags. Other choices of shape are semirectangular and rectangular. Most bags are constructed of nylon or nylon blends, inside and out. Sleeping bags with cotton insides, quilted rectangular shapes, or kiddy heroes printed on them are not recommended for backpacking or serious outdoor use.

THE RIGHT BACKPACK

There are hundreds of styles of backpacks on the market and everyone has a favorite, for an equal number of excellent reasons. Just because your best friend likes his, however, doesn't mean you will feel comfortable in it. Try on several backpacks and have the salesperson put 30 to 40 pounds in each one so you can walk around and compare them.

Internal-frame backpacks offer close fit, a low center of gravity, flexibility, and relative freedom of movement. The drawback with internal frames is that they do not carry unwieldy loads easily and can become quite unstable and uncomfortable if you end up lashing large amounts of gear to the outside of the pack.

External-frame backpacks are rigid, restrict movement, and have a higher center of gravity. Unlike an internal frame, however, the rigid frame can carry awkward loads quite comfortably and offers numerous points for lashing on extra items, which is useful for the parent who has to carry almost everything while the other parent carries the child.

Buying a backpack for a child is easier. I would recommend that children under eight years of age carry nothing more than a daypack. One with a waist strap will help to prevent the pack from bouncing around on your child's back.

As your child gets older and expresses an interest in carrying more (usually between the ages of eight and 10), it is time to consider buying a child-sized frame pack. Tough Traveler, JanSport, Kelty, Osprey, and Camptrails make good external-frame and internal-frame packs for children. The packs are adjustable to allow for the growth of the child. Avoid buying a pack that does not fit well and ends up bouncing and swaying around on your child's back. A loaded pack that does not fit is extremely uncomfortable and top-heavy. The predictable result is a miserable child and a ruined experience.

When the pack is loaded, the top of the shoulder straps and the bar they are attached to should rest between the top of the shoulders and the base of the skull. The waist belt should comfortably cup the hips, not so high that it compresses the stomach nor so low that it sits on the buttocks.

A GOOD STOVE

There was once a time when campfires were the way to cook, and you used a stove for convenience or backup. Now, however, firewood is becoming scarce in many camping sites and is sometimes nonexistent. With more people sharing and enjoying our wilderness heritage, cooking on stoves rather than on open fires becomes a much more ecologically responsible

Dressing in multiple layers is almost always better than dressing in one bulky jacket.

decision. Stoves leave no scarring fire rings, and no charred wood scattered around. And you do not have to worry about removing vital dead wood from the environment.

There are quite a number of backpacking stoves on the market but you are faced with one major choice: liquid fuel, such as white gasoline, or pressurized canister gas, such as butane or propane. White-gas stoves typically burn hotter than butane, will boil water faster, and can be pressurized with an external pump. On the down side, you have to prime white-gas stoves, the pumping can be a hassle, and they do require more frequent cleaning and maintenance. Butane stoves are more convenient to use. You turn on the gas and light it. But cold temperatures and a near-empty cartridge will render them less efficient.

A stove introduced by the Primus company in 1997 was advertised as being able to burn liquid and gas fuels. I would recommend you check it out in the store and ask for a demonstration. If it works as advertised, by all means spend the green! Before you leave the store, ask a salesperson to show you how to light and maintain your stove safely.

As I mentioned previously, never light a stove in a tent, and do not allow children to operate one unless they are supervised.

AN EFFICIENT KITCHEN

Assembling a kitchen kit is quite easy. With a few careful purchases, and some items borrowed from your home kitchen, you will be able to put together a very serviceable kit. Here's what you need:

POTS AND PANS. From a specialty outdoor store you will want to purchase a good set of nesting pots. I prefer stainless steel pots despite their extra weight because aluminum has been reported to harm the body over time. Aluminum pots also scratch, flake, and dent more easily. Mountain Safety Re-

> Cotton kills in cold weather. Once it is wet, it takes forever to dry, chills the skin, and opens the door wide to hypothermia.

search offers a new kit made of titanium, but I think it is far too expensive for most family groups and doesn't distribute the heat as well as stainless steel. Add a good pot grip, a mechanical handle that securely grabs the lip of each pot, a GI-issue folding can opener, and a Teflon frying pan with a folding handle and a lid. I also carry an Opinal folding knife that I use only for cooking. The blade stays extremely sharp and locks in place for security. It is inexpensive and light.

DON'T FORGET SPICES. For carrying spices, I would recommend buying a number of one-ounce Nalgene bottles with screw-on lids. Also, pick up a few one-ounce bottles with flip-top nozzles for liquids and oils. In Chapter 3, I'll discuss what to put in them.

SPOONS, SPATULA, AND A WHISK. From your home kitchen, select an old wooden spoon, a nylon spatula, and several small metal spoons. A tiny whisk is handy for mixing dried milk, pancake mix, hot cocoa, and so on. Lumpy drinks and food do not win over camp-food critics.

WHERE TO PUT IT ALL. Pack the pots in one stuffsack, the utensils in another smaller one, and the spices in a very small see-through ditty bag. The stuffsack for the pots will keep the inside of your backpack clean.

DON'T BURN YOUR FINGERS. If you plan to cook on a fire, add a pair of cotton or light leather gloves to your list. They will help prevent burns and definitely be worth the extra bulk and weight.

LEAVE THE FORK BEHIND. A knife, fork, and spoon are thought to be essential, but you can lighten your load if you reflect that a spoon can do almost everything a fork can do. I leave the fork at home. If each person is carrying a pocket knife, then there is also no need to pack along an extra knife just for eating.

PLATES, BOWLS, AND CUPS SHOULD BE LIGHT. The kit for each member of our family consists of a wide-bottomed cup and a plastic plate with deep sides that can double as a bowl. Children spill things very easily so whatever you choose, be sure that it is stable when full of food or drink. Also, the less a child has to hold or worry about, the less the likelihood of spillage.

DOUBLE-DUTY MEASURING CUPS. Take one or two of your camping cups and etch or mark measurements on the inside. I have marked ounces up the side of mine so that I can quite accurately measure ingredients in the field.

CHILD CARRIERS

Introducing children to the outdoors before they can walk any distance is a great way to get them excited about wilderness. It does, however, require that you act as mule and papoose carrier. The thought of adding extra and very shifty weight to your load sends shudders down the spine of many would-be camping parents. A word of comfort: The gentle rocking rhythm of a walking parent is often enough to put the squirmiest child to rest.

While a good child carrier is not cheap, it is worth its price for the comfort, support, and versatility provided to both parent and child. There are two basic types of carrier: the soft

A good child carrier is worth its price for the comfort, support, and versatility it gives to both child and parent.

snuggle sack that hangs in front of the parent, for children who are too young to sit up, and the framed carriers for older children up to 35 pounds.

The snuggle sack is probably best typified by the Snugli carrier. Its crisscross carrying design is quite comfortable. The baby is supported by an adjustable seat and rests inside a soft cotton-lined pouch. You wear the carrier slung in front for very young babies and over the back for larger infants. The main limitation is that its soft design affords no real support for the parent during long trips. I found this system ideal for my newborn, but quickly moved into something with more support once Nicole could sit up.

Larger frame-style child carriers come in a wide variety of designs and an equally wide variety of comfort levels. The way to decide what will work best for you and your child is to try the carriers, with the child on board, and compare the fit and feel. Your choices will vary from a simple plastic frame with minimal shoulder straps and a basic seat sling to intricate aluminum or composite frames with sturdy and well-padded suspensions similar to the most advanced expedition packs.

Most good child carriers are designed so the child is facing forward. This puts the child closer to your center of gravity, which translates into a more natural gait and stride for you. Since the child can easily see ahead, he or she will be more comfortable and more at ease, often putting a head on your shoulder to rest.

There are disadvantages to carrying children, however. One is the wandering little hands that love to pull your hair, stick fingers in your mouth, and inadvertently poke your eyes. Another is potentially dangerous. A child who is squirming and shifting, perhaps while turning around repeatedly to see a parent walking behind, creates an unwieldy load that can cause stumbles and make hiking less than pleasurable.

Nicole learned to shift her weight at calculated moments, causing Dad to stumble. It gave her thrill-a-minute giggles and Dad an extra rush of adrenaline. After one particularly close call where I nearly dived headfirst off the trail into a gully, Nicole was told in no uncertain terms that shifting and bouncing were not allowed.

Before you decide on a particular model, make sure the system you choose is sturdily built and comes with a safety belt to strap your child in. If you trip or fall, you could catapult an unbelted child into space, resulting in a nasty injury. Also,

Two items not to skimp on when purchasing equipment: boots and sleeping bag.

Inscribe gradations for measuring ingredients inside your camping cup.

choose a carrier with a built-in, fold-out stand that will support it upright on the ground. You will find this feature wonderful for quick rest stops although you should never leave your child unattended in a carrier. Finally, choose a carrier that has attached pockets and pouches for carrying extra gear and perhaps a place to secure a sleeping bag or two if needed. Tough Traveler, Madden, Lafuma, L.L. Bean, and Kelty all make good child carriers.

GEAR FOR KIDS

Children need special outfits. Your kids' needs will depend on several basic questions:

1. How young are your children?
2. What is your definition of dirty?
3. How much are you willing to carry?

Babies and toddlers need the most clothing because they are more likely to soil a garment inside and out. Stretchy one-piece suits are ideal for this age because they protect the entire body not only from the elements, but from insects as well. The older the child, the fewer changes he or she is likely to require, depending on your standards of cleanliness.

As a planning guide for teens I suggest one change of underwear and one pair of socks (liner and outer) for each day, plus one extra shirt, one extra pair of pants, a pair of shorts that will double as swim trunks.

For ages six to 12, plan on a fresh shirt for each day and add an extra pair of pants.

For children under six, I would plan on one complete outfit for each day plus several extra clean and warm outfits for sleeping and emergency ("How did you get *that* dirty?") use.

You should not ever need to pack more clothes than this, and if you can do with less, you will be the happier for it.

Three legs are better than two when crossing a stream. Use a long, sturdy stick—or, better, pack along a ski pole for such occasions.

DIAPERS ARE A PAIN IN THE WILDERNESS. But a necessary one. Some parents prefer cloth diapers and wash them when camping. They certainly are lighter and less bulky than disposables, but I hate washing dirty diapers and if the weather is wet, cloth diapers will not dry. Instead, I opt for disposables.

The major drawback with disposables is their weight once they have been used. You have to carry them out. Think of how much one soiled diaper weighs and then multiply that by the number of diapers your child uses per day. It's not light, that's for sure, and the bulk is somewhat daunting too. If you opt for disposable diapers, you will be limited to short backpacking jaunts.

Do not attempt to bury diapers, because the adverse environmental impact of this practice is not only ugly but permanent. While some parents have told me that it is possible to burn the fiber filling of the diaper (removing the plastic outer layer first) if your fire is hot enough, I would never recommend it. First, you'll need a fire so hot and so big that it just doesn't make environmental sense. The resulting odor is unpleasant and the fire must be carefully tended until the diaper is burned as completely as possible. And you'll still have to pack out any of the unburned remains. My preference is to bury the waste and pack out the diaper. Just as you would dispose of your own solid waste, bury the contents of the diaper four inches to six inches below the soil level. Double-bag the soiled diaper in a garbage sack and then put it in a large nylon stuff-sack that you can attach to the outside of your pack. The nylon stuffsack will protect the contents from ripping open and is easily hung when you are in bear country.

CLOTHING

Washing clothes will greatly reduce the number of extra outfits needed for your child, but there are some drawbacks. You will be dependent on warm, sunny weather to dry the clothes. If it is wet and the clothes do not dry, what then? Additionally, I do not enjoy being tied to a wash basin and clothesline. It is not my idea of an outdoor recreation. If you spend too much time performing chores, you end up with nothing more than a backwoods version of your normal housekeeping duties, which doesn't leave much time to truly enjoy the wilds and wonders you are trying to share.

The material and color of the clothing you choose is very important. Avoid the color blue as it does seem to attract mosquitoes and gnats more readily than other colors do. For younger children who are inclined to wander, select bright colors that are easily spotted. Choose synthetic materials whenever possible because they are lighter, provide excellent insulation, and dry out faster than their natural counterparts. Select materials made of pile, bunting, polypropylene, Capilene, Thermax, Polartec, and so on.

Natural fibers do work too, but you must understand their limitations. Cotton is great as a nonirritating fiber next to the skin and for keeping the body cool. It has no insulating value, however, since it absorbs moisture extremely well, and it takes forever to dry. So limit its use to warm weather. Wool is a su-

If you are sleeping cold, sleep in synthetic long underwear and a pair of synthetic socks. Still cold? Put on a rain suit as a vapor barrier over the underwear.

perb insulator, even when wet, but it does irritate the skin in many instances, leaving children and parents more frustrated than warm. Wool is probably best limited to socks and outerwear such as pants and sweaters.

When you are planning what your children will wear, think in terms of several layers. The first layer will be the wicking layer or underwear. This is followed by one or two insulating layers, depending on need: either a sweater or a jacket, or both. The final layer is the outer shell or protection from wind and rain. A carefully planned layering system will allow you to peel off or add clothing as your child's body temperature and environmental conditions dictate.

The inner layer is best made out of polypropylene, Thermax, or Capilene. A number of outdoor companies now make underwear for children. The insulating layer should consist of items such as a wool sweater, a wool or synthetic vest, a pile, or bunting jacket, or both vest and jacket. For the outer layer I would recommend a waterproof nylon jacket and pants. The rain-suit type of outerwear affords far more protection than a mere poncho and is a lot easier to romp and play in. Several companies make rain suits that reflect light for easy spotting at night—I like this feature.

When you are shopping for these various items, shock and horror may set in as you discover that the miniaturized versions cost just as much as the adult gear. Considering that your child will more than likely outgrow the outfit in a year or so, the economic implications might seem daunting. But that is not necessarily so. Not every item needs to come brand-new from the specialty outdoor retail store. The sale of used children's clothing is a growing business. You will find many items in flea markets and thrift shops. Quite a number of specialty stores hold big sales each year. Many of the same stores also have a bulletin board or other area in the store where used gear can be bought and sold. Some often-overlooked sources are friends and

> Biodegradable liquid dishwashing soap works just as well for your cleansing needs as does the more expensive "camper's soap."

other families with whom you can get acquainted through hiking clubs and camping groups.

Another way of extending your dollar value is to buy clothing with growth in mind. Most younger children tend to grow more in length than in width so do not be afraid to buy clothing a little long: you can always roll the excess up at the ankles or arms. Some manufacturers make clothes with growth adjustments built in. When buying pants, purchase those with adjustable or elastic waistbands.

FOOTWEAR

While some companies make special hiking boots for children, most children seem to prefer tennis shoes until they get older. I must admit, Nicole does like hiking boots. Putting on her boots makes her feel like an accomplished explorer ready for anything. As she got older, and as boots got lighter in weight, having a pair for romping and stomping became standard fare. Her favorite brands were Vasque, until she was eleven, and Timberland from then on.

While the debate over tennis shoes versus boots never stops, boots are the only appropriate choice when severe weather or rugged or snowy terrain are expected. If you buy boots for your child, make sure they are very comfortable. Most children's hiking boots are light in weight with a combination of nylon and leather uppers, and fairly flexible lug soles. Look for soles that offer a fair amount of friction so children will not slip or slide when they are running or jumping. Also, be sure your child is wearing the appropriate socks when you are trying boots for fit. Socks that are too thin will result in your buying boots too small. They are guaranteed to jam the toes and cramp the feet when thicker hiking socks are worn with them. The fit should be snug in the heel, roomy in the toes, and not binding. Do not buy a boot with the intention of having your child wear extra socks until he or she grows into them. To do so is asking for blisters and a ruined trip.

GEAR FOR BABIES

- A baby should wear a light-colored hat with a shade brim at all times. Some hats for babies come with a darker underside so that they don't reflect the bright sun into the infant's eyes.
- Be sure your child carrier comes with a sun shade. If it doesn't, make one by fastening a small umbrella to the carrier.
- Drape a hood of mosquito netting over the sun shade to prevent insects from chewing on your little darling.
- Don't put sunscreen or insect repellent on your infant's hands since it will always find its way into the mouth.
- Put sunscreen with a sun protection factor (SPF) of 25 or better on your child's face, arms, and legs, even if he or she is wearing long sleeves and pants. Sleeves and pant legs have a way of creeping up.
- If it's raining and you're still heading outdoors, be sure that your carrier has a waterproof hood. Simply dressing your child in a waterproof suit isn't sufficient.
- Remember that although you are moving, your passenger is not, so dress your child accordingly. Do not overdress them though. I have seen children sitting very unhappily in a child

> Headlamps are very useful. They beat the heck out of stuffing a flashlight in your mouth while fumbling around with your hands and trying to talk at the same time.

When you cross a stream, it is generally easier to wade across at its widest point—the water is flowing more slowly even though it may be deeper.

carrier, the victims of parents who felt that if one layer of clothes was good, two must be better.

The Theory of Layering

Layering enables you and your children to stay comfortable outdoors, no matter what the temperature or weather. Layers act as a protection against the sun when it's hot, against the rain when it pours, and against the cold when the temperature dips.

The basics are quite simple. As you warm up, you peel off layers, as you cool down, you add layers. Follow these simple guidelines for maximum comfort:

IS IT HOT AND SUNNY? Choose long- or short-sleeved shirts of loose cotton or cotton/synthetic blend material. Loose-fitting pants or shorts with a built-in mesh brief are best. Don't wear cotton briefs because they chafe. Bring along a lightweight fleece jacket and a light-colored windproof/water-resistant shell. Top off your noggin with a light-colored hat. Socks should be synthetic or wool, not cotton.

IS IT WARM NOW, BUT LIKELY TO COOL DOWN LATER? MAYBE A HINT OF RAIN? Wear a lightweight, synthetic, long underwear top. If you get cold easily, add the bottoms too. Choose loose-fitting shorts or long pants and a short-sleeved T-shirt of cotton/synthetic blend.

As you get cool, toss on a midweight fleece pullover or woollen sweater. Light fleece pants will take the chill off your legs.

If the wind blows, slip into a waterproof/breathable shell jacket and add the pants for extra protection. A baseball cap tops off the ensemble. Pack along a woollen cap just in case.

IS THERE A CHILL TO THE AIR, PERHAPS A DUSTING OF SNOW ON THE GROUND? Wear lightweight synthetic long underwear, tops and bottoms. Add a midweight or expedition-weight synthetic underwear top for extra warmth. Still cold? Put on a light fleece jacket and fleece pants. Need more insulation? Add a synthetic or down parka large enough to accommodate all the layers underneath. Is the wind cutting through you? Slip into a waterproof/breathable-shell mountain parka and shell pants with side-zip entry. Add gaiters to keep the snow out of your boots. You will need an insulated hat, either wool or synthetic (I prefer fleece bomber hats). Insulated gloves or mittens are a must. If it is really cold, you will want to protect your head and face with a synthetic balaclava.

The Ten Essentials

"Ten Essentials" is the term coined by The Mountaineers, a nonprofit outdoor publisher and club, to describe the equipment you need to survive an emergency in the wilderness. The original 10 have since expanded on many lists to include some items of rudimentary comfort and not just survival (for example, toilet paper.)

The original Ten Essentials are:

Topographic map
Compass
Flashlight with extra bulb and batteries
Extra food
Extra clothing, including rain gear
Sunglasses and sunscreen

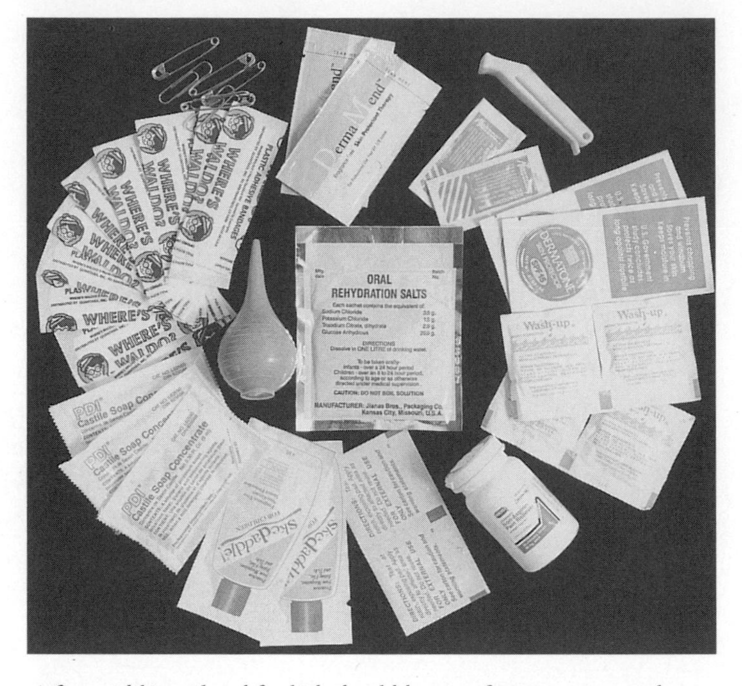

A first-aid kit tailored for kids should be one of your ten essentials.

Pocket knife
Waterproof matches
Firestarter or candle
First-aid kit

Other pieces of equipment that are strongly recommended and begin to expand the list are: water bottle, ground insulation (such as an Ensolite pad), emergency blanket, tub shelter or rain fly, signaling devices (such as signal flares, mirror, and whistle.)

Your list of essentials may grow as your family needs dictate. Your choice will also depend on what kind of activity you undertake. Different items are needed for backpacking, canoeing, bicycling, and cross-country skiing.

Tips in a Nutshell

1. Find out what's available, using catalogs, magazines such as *Backpacker* or *Outside*, friends' opinions, and advice from a specialty store.
2. Rent whenever you can—many specialty stores will rent tents, backpacks, sleeping bags, stoves, and even child carriers. Avoid renting boots.
3. Ignore discount store prices and buy quality whenever the budget will allow.
4. Borrow old cookware from your home kitchen. Leave forks at home, take just spoons. Be sure that bowls for children are sturdy and won't tip easily.
5. Always pack and carry the Ten Essentials.
6. Be sure your child carrier can stand on its own, is comfortable for you and the child, has a seat belt, and is sturdily built.
7. Never bury diapers outdoors. Always carry out what you carry in. Many parents use cloth diapers, but the washing and drying can be tiresome.
8. Select bright clothing to keep your children visible. Stay away from the color blue as it seems to attract mosquitoes and gnats. Choose synthetic materials such as pile, polypropylene, Capilene, bunting, Thermax, and Synchilla. They dry quicker than natural fibers.
9. Always layer: the first layer is underwear; the second layer is made up of a number of insulating layers depending on need; the third layer consists of rain wear for protection against wind and showers.
10. Most younger children seem to prefer tennis shoes to hiking boots. Boots are appropriate if weather or difficult hiking conditions dictate more foot protection—for example, snow, loose rocks, and wet or muddy terrain. When fitting boots, children should wear the socks they will be hiking in. Do not buy boots for the child to grow into. That is asking for blisters and misery.

CHAPTER 3

Planning the Camping Trip

PLANNING IS AN IMPORTANT PHASE FOR CHILDREN TO BE involved in if they are to become part of the adventure. In the long run, it is important for you to spend the extra minutes it will take to teach children how to repackage food, how to lay out gear so they can see what they are packing, how to load a pack, and how to check equipment for safety and function. If a parent assumes all the tasks, there's a good chance the trip will become drudgery for the parent and boring for the children.

Choosing the Destination

Even if you have successfully completed every preparatory step, from the backyard camp-out and state park day hikes to camping overnight, you can't predict everything that will happen when you take your family on an extended camping trip for the first time. Nevertheless, while flexibility and a positive attitude are obviously important, proper planning and the choice of an appropriate destination should be your major objectives. They are your first line of defense against unexpected trouble.

Spend as much time as you can with the family poring over all the information available about areas you want to

Look for a trip that will excite and challenge your kids.

visit. Magazines, books, park flyers, travelogues, and state or provincial promotional brochures are all excellent resources. Appendix II lists magazines that will prove useful. For detailed guidebooks, try your local specialty outdoor store's book department.

To make this process most productive, you and your family must ask yourselves a number of questions. What are your activity interests—fishing, hiking, scrambling, climbing, swimming? How important is viewing wildlife—deer, bear, squirrels, skunks, raccoons? Will studying the stars or viewing vast fields of wildflowers be important? What is the maximum hiking distance your family can easily handle? How near to the parking area or car do you wish to be in case of emergencies?

Learn to tie a few basic knots—half-hitch, tautline hitch, clove hitch, and the trucker's hitch.

What kind of temperatures and weather are you likely to encounter—foggy, sunny, rainy, snowy, a variety? What is the terrain like—rolling, flat, mountainous, swampy? Is your family interested in history, such as the Yukon Gold Rush, the Donner Party, the Cumberland Gap? Once you have answered these and any other questions you deem important to your family, then the planning can begin in earnest.

One other question that should not be overlooked: How long and how difficult is the drive to and from the chosen site? This may not seem like a major consideration until you've tried sitting in a car for more than four hours with children craving and counting on activity. It's a recipe for frustration, irritation, and possibly the worst question you could hear from your children: "I hate this, why didn't we just stay home?" It's not an ideal way to begin a family outing to the wilderness.

Once your family has decided on a potential area, from reading and researching, try talking to people who have been there. Find out from them what the area is really like. Firsthand experience is invaluable for obtaining specific information such as the location of hidden hot springs, the best place to fish, the ideal campsite, seasonal insect populations, precautions you need to take against bears or other animals, the difficulty of terrain, and so on.

Finally, after all the information has been digested, and you have tentatively selected a destination, think about your family's physical and emotional abilities. Be very honest. Is the destination feasible and is it a good choice for fun and safety? If the answer remains yes, your destination is locked in and equipment planning begins.

If the answer is no, or you're not sure, pick something a little less ambitious for this first trip. You can always progress later to the one you really wanted to go on and it will probably be that much more enjoyable then.

Once the destination has been fixed, you will need detailed information. This involves purchasing United States Geological Survey (USGS) topographic survey maps for the area, National Forest Service maps, trail guide books, and privately produced maps of the area if available. You cannot have too much information in this planning stage. Of course, you will probably only pack along the topographic maps, and maybe the guidebook if it is small enough. Appendix VI lists addresses and sources for this type of information.

Plot your route carefully on the maps. Many of the USGS topo maps were last surveyed in the 1950s; revisions and updates (often checked only by aerial survey) are slow in coming. Transcribing detailed information on trails, roads, and other man-made landmarks from Forest Service maps, private maps, and guidebooks to the topos is most helpful. If you are lucky, the private maps will be reproductions of the USGS maps with all the necessary trail and hiking data updated and transcribed for you.

Checking Equipment

Our family finds it helpful to lay out all equipment in plain view on the living room floor. While this tends to make the room look like the site of a small nuclear explosion, it does serve

Know how to take apart and field-repair all your equipment—especially your stove.

to keep all items in plain view, making it easy to see if we have everything necessary for the trip. As one of us calls out the items on the checklist, someone puts that item to one side in the room, ready to be checked and packed.

And believe me, all equipment does get checked. Pots are checked for cleanliness; stoves for fuel and function (a stove that will not light is more easily repaired at home); flashlights for power; knives for sharpness; tent for tears and dirt; sleeping bags for good loft, cleanliness, and tears; sleeping pads for air leaks; and packs for tears and cracked frames. The first-aid kit requires special checking to be sure that the contents are not outdated, that all materials are clean, and that any items previously used have either been replaced or sterilized.

Finally, with everything except food spread out in an orderly fashion on the floor, we go through the list to determine if we are leaving anything out or if we are packing too much. Always operate under the KISS principle—Keep It Simple, Stupid. Pack and carry as little as necessary to be comfortable and safe. If in doubt, leave it behind. Don't duplicate.

EMERGENCY REPAIRS

Murphy's Law works well in the wilds. Leave your raincoat at home and presto, a downpour. Forget your stove repair kit and your stove breaks down. The answer is good planning and a good field repair kit.

After years of working as a professional mountain guide, in search-and-rescue expeditions, and as a product tester, I have devised a basic repair kit for emergencies. This is what it contains:

- Duct tape for patching holes, splinting tent poles, repairing boots, and dozens of similar repairs.
- A Leatherman tool, available from REI and other specialty stores, that comprises a knife, pliers, and other useful tools in one compact kit.

- Sandpaper for roughing up surfaces I may have to glue together.
- Seam Grip, a new waterproof, urethane-rubber compound that works as a seam sealer and patching compound.
- A spare flashlight, batteries, and bulb.
- Miscellaneous spare parts for the stove.
- Waxed thread (like dental floss) and needles (one medium-sized and one leather needle) for repairs to leather and webbing.
- A spare, 1-inch nylon strap with buckle.
- A tent-pole sleeve—a standard 3-inch, heavy-gauge, aluminum tube that joins broken tent poles.

As each trip demands repair items specific to that trip (a backcountry ski trip requires binding parts for skis, splint material for poles, and a spare ski tip), I evaluate the basic kit and make necessary adjustments. As for the weight of the kit, I try to keep it between 1 pound and 1½ pounds. That's not light, admittedly, but I'll take a pound of prevention over a ton of misery any day.

My friend Mark Jenkins, an experienced outdoorsman, suggests that you might want to carry some additional items on any prolonged trip into the hinterlands. Jenkins urges packing a 5-inch by 5-inch patch of mosquito netting for the one time a hole appears in your tent screening, and 5 inches of 1-inch-wide Velcro, with adhesive coating on the back sides of both the hooks and loops, for repairing jackets or sleeping bags if the zippers give out. He also advises packing several hose clamps for splinting a broken backpack frame.

N W E S

If you see berry bushes in bear country, expect to see bears also.

Many repair kits include rubber bands for securing equipment. I used to pack several heavyweight ones myself. But Pat McHugh, who has extensive knowledge of outdoor safety products, suggests the substitution of large-sized, 25-cent balloons for rubber bands, and he makes a good case. The elasticity of a large balloon allows you to lash poles together for an emergency shelter. Balloons can be used as tent tie-down lines. They can secure gear in a canoe, or to a backpack. If you partially inflate the balloon, it becomes a makeshift pillow.

The bottom line is that you should assemble a repair kit to meet your needs. Use your imagination and the basic guidelines I have offered and plan for the unexpected because you can bet that the one time you aren't ready for the unexpected is the one time the unexpected will happen to you. In the wilderness, after all, you can't call for a repair person; you will have to make do yourself.

Planning the Menu

When you are putting together a menu for your trip, don't overlook the importance of taste, nutrition, and energy content. Adults and children need high-energy carbohydrate foods when adventuring outdoors. This is not to say that your family's diet should become one of sugar and fat during a wilderness excursion. Meals and snacks that include pasta, milk, cheese, rice, seeds, nuts, dried fruit, and vegetables will adequately meet nutritional needs for yourself and the children in your family. You also need to consider weight, ease of packaging and handling, and variety.

Water is critical to menu planning. It is vital that each person in your family drink 2 to 4 quarts of water a day. Just as important is the need to maintain the body's balance of water and salt. The normal diet includes adequate salt without your having to be concerned about adding more, but if the trip is extremely difficult or the weather unusually hot, then it's appropriate to add an electrolyte to the water. Be careful not to overdo the salt intake, however, because too much salt is more harmful than too little. Proper hydration will help to prevent hypothermia, heat stroke, heat cramps, frostbite, and altitude sickness. If there's no water along the way, be sure to take it with you.

You can reduce weight by combining dried, dehydrated, and freeze-dried foods along with any fresh selections in your menu. Further lighten your load by repacking everything into Ziploc plastic bags. Choose sturdy, freezer-quality Ziploc bags and not flimsy sandwich ones. Stay away from canned goods.

I have found it more convenient and more efficient to prepackage meals into large freezer-variety Ziploc bags. If it is possible, I premeasure and premix all the dry ingredients in the same bag. Don't forget to label the bag and, unless you have an incredible memory, drop in briefly written preparation instructions with each meal.

Spoilage is a problem when you do not have a cooler. For this reason, do not take real butter, fresh meats, eggs, or bacon. Most cheeses are fine outdoors and will not spoil, but

Well-fed children are happy children.

"Water is Life!" Nothing could be more simple or true. Two to four quarts of water per day per person is a minimum. More at altitude or in the cold.

some processed cheeses deteriorate quickly and should be avoided. Hard, aged cheeses will usually hold up better than soft cheeses. Jarlsberg and Gouda are two of my favorites.

The rule is to plan your meals and snacks so they will be easy and fun to prepare, look appealing, and be tasty. The following list will help you plan your own menus, but don't forget to ask for your children's suggestions as well.

BREAKFAST

Drinks: cocoa, orange juice crystals, Tang, tea, coffee, low-fat dried milk

Cereal: oatmeal, Cream of Wheat, Malto Meal, Cream of Rice, granola, 7-grain, and muesli

Main dishes: pancake mix (Bisquick works great), and western omelet (freeze-dried)

Dried fruit: apricots, prunes, raisins, apples, pineapples, plums, cherries, pears, and peaches

TRAIL LUNCHES

Meat: bacon bits or bar, jerky (beef or turkey), salami, pemmican, and beef stick

Cheese: any nonpasteurized nonprocessed cheese that does not require refrigeration

Nuts: peanuts, pecans, cashews, pine nuts, walnuts, hazelnuts and almonds

Seeds: pumpkin, sunflower, soya, and sesame

Fresh vegetables: carrots, radishes, cauliflower, jicama, celery, turnips, and broccoli

Fresh fruits: apples, oranges, and tangerines

Dried or freeze-dried fruits: dates, apples, pineapple, bananas, peaches, prunes, apricots, and raisins

Breads/crackers/pastries: Lebanese flat bread, sourdough, rye, pilot biscuits, Ritz, Waverly, Triscuits, Rye-Crisps, Japanese rice crackers, Cheese Nips, melba toast, trail biscuits, Pop-Tarts, and Danish

Sweets: licorice, Tootsie Rolls, lemon drops, candy orange slices, tropical chocolate, malted milk tablets, Life Savers, fruit bars or rollups, sesame seed bars, puddings (various flavors in small aluminum cans, but pack out the cans), and cookies

Drinks: Kool-Aid, Wylers, juice crystals, Tang, hot cocoa (nothing better on a cold day), and individual-serving-size boxes of juice

DINNERS

Drinks: Wylers, Kool-Aid, tea, coffee, hot cocoa, and Tang

Soups: Lipton and Knorr instants, Top Ramen (freeze-dried from outdoor specialty store)

Freeze-dried dinners: Richmoor, Natural High, Backpacker Pantry, AlpineAire, Weepak, and Mountain House (If you have never tried freeze-dried dinners, buy several, take them home, and prepare them. I must admit a preference for Backpacker Pantry desserts and side dishes, and AlpineAire and Natural High main courses)

MEAL STAPLES AND MIXES

Textured vegetable protein made of soy bean and good for soups or casseroles

Uncle Ben's Quick Brown Rice

Bisquick

Pastas

Lentils, pinto beans, and Lima beans

Corn-bread mixes
Instant potatoes
Miso instant gravy or sauce packets, in tomato, chicken, and beef flavors
Freeze-dried chicken
Freeze-dried vegetables

SPICES AND ADDITIVES

Cinnamon sugar—sprinkle on cereal, hot biscuits, pancakes, and so on
Squeeze Parkay, Country Crock, or other margarine
Crisco, in small container. Better than oils and butter for cooking and frying and it doesn't burn or break down as easily on a hot flame. After each use, pour back into container and reuse
Honey—healthier than white sugar for sweetening. Package in a squeeze tube or 8-ounce Nalgene bottle
Peanut butter and honey mix—premix two parts peanut butter to one part honey and package in squeeze tube. Add more honey to soften consistency.
Brown sugar—less messy alternative to honey
Dry milk—Milkman low-fat milk for flavoring and mixes. Make into a paste before adding water to help prevent lumps
Cinnamon, nutmeg, curry, oregano, chili powder, garlic, black pepper, salt, dry mustard—package each in one-ounce Nalgene bottles and label
Soy sauce—the backpackers' ketchup

Repackage store-bought food into reusable containers to reduce waste.

Worcestershire sauce and Tabasco sauce—package in flip-top bottles for spicing up otherwise bland freeze-dried meals
Bouillon cubes or powder

MY FAVORITE MEALS

Breakfast: Pancakes and wild berry syrup, hot cocoa or orange juice crystals, and dried fruit
Lunch: Gorp, peanut butter and honey mix on Ritz crackers or party rye bread, beef jerky, Wylers lemonade mix or water, candy bar
Dinner: Freeze-dried spaghetti mix, Knorr instant vegetable soup, instant chocolate pudding using instant milk, Tang, Wylers, or water

GREAT HOMEMADE SNACKS

After four years as a camp counselor and camp trip director, five years as a mountain guide and outings program director, 15 years as a parent taking my daughter and her friends on outings, and seven years taking my daughter to summer camp and swapping ideas with other parents, I have learned what kids like and don't like. You and your family should find in this chapter some snacks you'll enjoy making and munching on. Here is a collection of my favorite recipes and snacks that you can make before hitting the trail. Enjoy!

TRAIL MIX. For the best trail mix, I suggest you head directly to a health food store or a specialty food store. Typically, these stores have large bins full of tasty trail mixes alongside other bins of dried fruits, nuts, seeds, and so on. Begin with a basic mix, such as a tropical blend with premixed bits of nuts, papaya, coconut, and raisins, and then add other ingredients to your heart's content. I never pass up an opportunity to add butterscotch chips to my mix. As for estimating how much you will need, I have found that about one-half pound of trail mix

Never let your water bottle run dry. Take the time to top it off at every opportunity.

You can never find too many uses for duct tape—always pack some along.

per person per eight-hour hiking day does the trick quite nicely. If you and your family want to try something truly exotic, then taste-test the following:

Blend together two cups of cereal (containing flakes, bits of fruit and nuts), with one cup of chopped walnuts, one cup of sunflower seeds, one cup of golden raisins, and two cups of bittersweet chocolate chips (my daughter and I prefer Giardelli's brand). You can also substitute or experiment by blending in butterscotch or peanut-butter chips. Heat over a stove or in a microwave until the chips melt. Stir the ingredients until they are all well coated with melted chips. Spread the mixture out on a well-greased cookie sheet and form it into a flat sheet about 2 inches thick. Chill the sheet, cut into squares, and wrap in plastic for your hike.

PEANUT BRITTLE. I love peanut brittle. It's a high-energy snack that goes a long way to restoring flagging spirits on the trail. It's practically indestructible, even if it does get a little tacky when it's hot. You can buy it at any candy store, but it's a lot more fun to make your own and making it is quite easy, as you'll find out when you try to make it. Just follow the recipe on page 45. A note on the "peanut" in peanut brittle: Tradition calls for 2 cups of peanuts to be added, but I prefer to use 2 cups of mixed nuts, including chopped walnuts, pecans, and cashews.

2 cups sugar
1 cup light corn syrup
1 cup water
2 cups unroasted peanuts (or mixed nuts)
1/4 teaspoon salt
1 teaspoon butter or margarine
1/4 teaspoon soda

Combine sugar, corn syrup, and water in heavy skillet. Cook slowly, stirring till sugar dissolves. Cook to soft-ball stage (test a few drops in cold water).

Add peanuts and salt. Cook to hard-crack stage, stirring constantly (remove candy from heat while testing). Add butter and soda; stir to blend. (Mixture will bubble.)

Pour onto buttered large plates or platters. Cool partially by lifting around edges with spatula. Keep spatula moving under mixture so it won't stick. When it's firm but still warm, turn it over; pull edges to make brittle thinner in center. Break in pieces when cold.

JERKY. Although drying jerky and other foods works best if you own a dryer designed for the purpose, an ordinary oven will serve well. Beef or turkey jerky is a wonderful treat. Homemade jerky is so superior in quality and flavor to most commercial brands, and so easy to make, that I wonder why more hikers don't make it. My favorite cut of meat for jerky is flank steak. You can figure that 3 pounds of meat will yield about 1 pound of jerky.

Before you begin slicing, firm the meat in the freezer—your cuts will be more even. Remove excess fat. Then, slice the meat across the grain to a thickness of between 1/8 and 1/4 of an inch. Marinate the sliced meat overnight in a refrigerator in a tightly sealed container. I prefer a teriyaki marinade, which you can make easily enough by taking one cup of soy sauce, ½ cup of dark-brown sugar, 2 teaspoons of ginger, 4 to 6 cloves of crushed garlic, and ½ teaspoon of freshly ground black pepper.

Spray your oven racks with a vegetable spray and then spread the strips of meat across the rack. Be sure to place a sheet of aluminum foil over the bottom of the oven to catch the drips, otherwise you will make an awful mess. Unless your oven is very well calibrated, a portable thermometer may be useful. The ideal temperature for drying meat is about 140°F. This temperature is usually toward the middle setting of the warm label on the oven knob. Prop the oven door open a few inches, using a pot lid or something non-flammable, so that the moisture will escape easily from the drying meat. Your jerky should be ready in approximately 8 hours—it should be dry, but not brittle to the touch.

FRUIT LEATHER. When I'm trekking in the desert, I love to nibble on good fruit leather. It tastes great, won't spoil, and won't make you feel extra thirsty. Like jerky, fruit leather is most easily made in a dehydrator, but your kitchen oven will do just fine. To make fruit leather, spray a large cookie sheet with a vegetable spray or coat it lightly with vegetable oil. Puree the fresh fruit of your choice (I am partial to peach, apricot, nectarine, and apple) in a blender until it is smooth—no lumps, wayward seeds, or other items to mess up the consistency. If the fruit puree is not sweet enough for you, add white corn syrup (or honey, if you prefer) to taste. Do not use sugar as it will only make the leather grainy and brittle. Add a few drops of lemon juice to enhance the fruit flavor. Pour the puree onto the greased cookie sheet to an even thickness of about ¼ inch. Place the cookie sheet into an oven set to 140°F.

Once again, prop the oven door open a few inches, using

Unbuckle the waist belt and sternum strap and loosen the shoulder straps of your pack before crossing a stream.

a pot lid or something nonflammable, so that the moisture will escape easily from the drying puree. The fruit leather is correctly dried when it is pliable but not sticky. Peel it gradually off the cookie sheet and roll it into one large roll as you go. Cut the giant roll into 4- to 5-inch-long sections. Wrap each section in plastic and keep it cool until you are ready to hit the trail. Yummy!

APPLE OR APRICOT FRUIT CHEW. When you're wandering through the woods, there is nothing quite as good as a flavorful fruit-and-nut treat followed by a cool water chaser. Making your own fruit treat is easy if you follow the recipe shared with me by a client when I was guiding backpacking trips in Southern California many years ago.

Mix 2 cups of finely chopped and dried apples, 2 cups of finely chopped and dried apricots, and ½ cup instant dried milk (nonfat, if you like).

Add 4 tablespoons of frozen fruit juice concentrate (I prefer apple or orange), 2 teaspoons of cinnamon, 4 tablespoons of honey and 4 tablespoons of light corn syrup.

Roll the mixture into one long fruit log about 1 inch to 1½ inches in diameter. If you wish—and I highly recommend it—roll the entire log over 1 or 2 cups of chopped walnuts, and then through powdered sugar to coat the fruit thoroughly with a sweet-and-nut topping. Dry the entire mess at a temperature of about 140°F until firm, remembering to leave the oven door ajar to allow moisture to escape. When the log is firm, take it out of the oven, allow it to cool, and then slice it into 1-inch-thick sections. Wrap each section in plastic and hit the trail.

REPACKAGING FOOD

If you don't yet own stock in the Ziploc corporation, consider buying some. Self-sealing plastic bags are a camper's best friend. Much of your food, with the exception of fresh produce, should get repackaged into them. Fresh produce is best carried in a porous mesh bag carried near the top of a pack, or outside it, as produce tends to spoil in plastic unless it is refrigerated.

I pack bulk foods and frequently used foods in double freezer bags or 1-quart Nalgene bottles with wide mouths. For beverages, sugar, milk, and coffee, I prefer wide-mouth Nalgene bottles. They are easier to open and close frequently, are more easily handled by little hands, and won't tear or break. Food items such as Bisquick, flour, pasta, and dried fruits will pack handily in a double-bag system. I recommend double bagging to prevent accidental bursting and puncturing in your pack.

Setting up a small assembly line, with your spouse and/or older children performing the measuring tasks and writing of labels, is quite an efficient and pleasant method of repackaging foods and meals. The younger children will enjoy sealing the bags (be sure they squeeze out all of the air) and sticking on the labels.

If you would like a little fresh food on your outing, why not grow sprouts? You can get seeds and directions from a health-food store. The basic idea is to take some alfalfa seeds, place them in a small sealable plastic bag, keep the seeds moist, and rinse with fresh water every day. Each child can be put in charge of cultivating a plastic-bag garden. They will enjoy watching the seeds sprout in their packs on the trip.

Packing the Gear

Packing isn't as difficult as you might imagine. With all the gear still laid out on the living room floor, and the food arranged by meals and days, begin loading the packs. The rough rule of thumb is to keep heavier items close to your center of gravity, your back, and not too high or too low in the pack. For men this is usually higher on the back next to the shoulders. Women will tend to be more comfortable by packing heavier weight lower and more towards the middle of the pack—just above the small of the back and next to the frame. Work your way out with medium-weight items and then finally place the lightest items in the most distant corners of your pack.

Children should be carefully supervised when loading their packs. Smaller, younger children want to be involved, but should not be allowed to carry more than two or three small and fairly lightweight items. Older children will be able to carry more, but beware of turning them into pack mules, and restricting their freedom to play and romp. Remember why you are heading into the wilderness with them in the first place.

Teenagers should be allowed to carry more, but be careful of their egos. Some children will attempt to carry too much in order to impress others and may end up exhausting or injuring themselves. Other children may begin to feel very self-conscious about not being allowed to carry what they perceive to be their fair share. This is a very vulnerable age and emotions must be handled tenderly. I have found it most effective to play down the importance of carrying large loads and, instead, to emphasize certain wilderness skills that anyone can acquire. Of these skills, the most important are building

Take the time to learn cardiopulmonary resuscitation (CPR).

campfires, reading maps, preparing food, and weather forecasting. It doesn't particularly matter who can carry the heaviest load. When I worked as a camp counselor, I found that if teenagers were gung-ho about carrying a large load, I reacted by unloading my pack on them. They soon discovered that carrying an extra-heavy load was neither desirable nor rewarding.

The younger the children, the more of their burden the parents must shoulder. It often happens that one parent will carry the bulk of the family gear and food while the other parent carries a child and whatever equipment is left over. But if one parent is left carrying a ridiculously heavy, awkward load, I would recommend hiking only a short way to a wilderness base camp. Once at the base camp, your family can continue to enjoy a wide and varied wilderness experience by going on day hikes. If necessary, you can still hike to the vehicles to pick up cached gear or food.

Being Prepared

A ready-packed camping kit in your car or garage gives you a head start on any trip. I learned long ago, from a Scoutmaster friend who had to manage not only his own family of five but his troop of 15, that you can give the illusion of spontaneous camping decisions as long as you subscribe to the car camping–prepacked-box method. If you have all the necessities already packed and ready to go at a moment's notice, all you need to do is determine the destination and find the kids.

I keep all the items in a large plastic cargo box, next to the large cooler in the garage. Here are the contents of my box, but feel free to modify this list to meet your own needs:

Non-stick skillet, large pot, small pot, two-burner stove, spatula, pot grips, plastic cutting board, 9-inch slicing and chopping knife, multitool knife, small paring knife, plastic plates, plastic cups, plastic knife, fork, and spoon sets, camp-

Camping with children dictates that you allow for lots of time to explore, romp, and splash along the way.

ing hammock, oven mitts, water filter, first-aid kit, spice kit, roll of paper towels, can opener, barbecue tongs and fork, matches, resealable plastic bags, large garbage bags, water filter, 5-gallon water jug, aluminum foil, tablecloth, sponge, camp soap, dishwashing basin, dishtowel, lantern, flashlight, extra batteries, folding chairs, duct tape, 50 feet of nylon cord, an assortment of bungee cord, a 12-foot by 12-foot heavyweight plastic tarp, sleeping pads, camp tent, frisbee, Nerf balls, football, playing cards, and travel games set.

The Child's Point of View

The importance of keeping the children in mind when you are planning a trip has already been stressed. But it may help if you know, from the very beginning, what kids like and don't like. The following lists, collected over the years, contain tips that may help you see a little deeper into your child's mind, and to understand better his or her reactions on the trail. Of course, there is no suggestion that you should refrain from applying sunscreen just because your child thinks it's "goopy," nor should you take too seriously their criticism that telling them what to bring is treating them like 2-year-olds. The value of these lists is that they emphasize sensitive areas, areas of potential conflict, that might benefit from cautious handling with the advantage of foreknowledge.

THE BEST THINGS ABOUT CAMPING

1. The food tastes better
2. I don't have to worry about staying clean

3. Staying up late
4. Sleeping under the stars
5. Fresh air
6. It's peaceful
7. Seeing wildlife
8. It's never boring

THE WORST THINGS ABOUT CAMPING

1. Mosquitoes
2. Ticks
3. Noisy, drunk people
4. Bears and trash
5. Nagging parents
6. Park ranger trucks kicking up dust
7. Rain
8. Burned food
9. Sleeping cold
10. Going to the bathroom at night in the cold and dark

WHY PARENTS DRIVE US NUTS!

1. Going to the next camp to ask for toilet paper
2. Spraying bug repellent all over us
3. Covering us with goopy sunscreen that just collects dirt
4. Cramming the whole family into one tent to save money
5. Telling us what to bring as if we were 2 years old
6. Taking surprise photographs
7. Making us eat gross camping food like packaged chili and stuff
8. Hiking too fast
9. Hiking too far
10. Getting too enthusiastic
11. Camp is never "around the next corner!"
12. Spending forever talking to people along the trail and in camp so you never get to where you are going in time

Tips in a Nutshell

1. Remain flexible, be positive, plan well.
2. Use magazines, guidebooks, park flyers, promotional brochures, and travelogues to help you plan your destination. Always involve the entire family in the planning process. Additional and valuable sources of information are USGS topographical maps, Forest Service maps, and privately produced maps.
3. Determine family needs and interests—fishing, hiking, scrambling, climbing, swimming, wildlife observation, history, and so on.
4. Keep driving distances to and from the chosen destination to a minimum. Four hours is long enough in a car if you expect the children to be eager about the hike.
5. Check all equipment carefully before heading into the field. A stove is more easily repaired at home than in the wilderness.
6. Plan your menus considering taste, nutrition, energy, ease of packaging, ease of handling, variety, and spoilage. Involve children in the menu planning and include some of their favorite foods.
7. Plan on 2 to 4 quarts of water per person per day.
8. Combine freeze-dried, dehydrated, dried, and fresh foods to keep weight to a minimum. Also, remove all food from cans, bottles, and boxes, and repack into sealable plastic bags.
9. Growing alfalfa sprouts in a plastic bag is fun for the children, and a source of fresh food.
10. Distribute loads as fairly as possible. Avoid one parent becoming pack mule for the clan. Keep children's packs light and discourage teenagers from taking on too much.

CHAPTER 4

The Family Camping Trip

ONCE YOU HAVE LEFT YOUR CAR AND BEGUN THE WALK TO camp, motivational challenges may crop up. Children's minds tend to wander, and if they are not entertained the sameness and perceived drudgery of hiking will probably turn into a continual and very irritating whining. Although playing games and providing entertainment for children is not why most adults head into the wilderness, try to remember that you are striving to create a positive and enticing atmosphere.

If heading up a hill chugging like a train and pulling on an imaginary whistle works, go for it. Singing songs, playing I Spy, fantasizing that you are on a secret exploration, or pointing out interesting animal signs, are all techniques successfully used by parents and camp counselors. Remember that while you may hit on an idea that will work well for 20 minutes or so, nothing works forever or every time. Use variety and capitalize on a child's wonderful imagination.

Children tend to hike in rapid spurts, so keep the hiking pace slow and steady enough that they don't wear out their tiny legs too soon. As you walk along, use generous amounts of encouragement and keep telling your children how well they are doing and how far they have come.

Favorite treats are often used to motivate little hikers, but I try to play this down, and I rarely practiced it with my own child. This attitude seems to border on buying behavior, and encourages eating as a reward. This is not to belittle the need for tasty or regular food breaks, but with my family they are just that—regular food breaks and not something I use to get junior to walk from point A to B in a pinch.

Try to keep your breaks frequent. On the average, plan on a rest every 30 minutes. Packs come off, snacks come out, water is passed around, and children should be encouraged to sit and rest. You will often find that children enjoy being the leader of a group. Put them in front of the pack and allow them to lead you up the trail and to set the pace. I have found that even very tired children will perk up and stride along happily when put in front, but make sure the child's sudden enthusiasm for leading does not translate into a short-lived and maniacal pace.

Even spectacular scenery won't hold your child's interest for long. Take frequent breaks.

Most often, a stove is better than a fire. Fires scar the land, use up wood, and ruin your night vision.

Setting Up Camp

Setting up a campsite can be a wonderful family activity, but if your children are genuinely too tired to help, they are better off being left to play and rest quietly. Be sure to establish firm boundaries around camp immediately, beyond which they are not to go without a parent. You should look out for poisonous plants, steep banks by a river's edge, loose rocks near a cliff edge, dead trees that might topple, and so on. Be sure your children are aware of any dangers. Also, be sure not to set up camp beside or directly under any of the aforementioned hazards.

If it has been raining, or is somewhat cold, the first task should be to set up the tent and get the family dry and warm. Almost at the same time, you will want to get a fire or stove going for hot drinks. There is nothing like hot chocolate or even hot flavored gelatin to put the sparkle back in a child's eye.

I carry an extra 9-foot by 9-foot nylon tarp with grommets on the sides and at the corners, and 50 feet of extra cord. In the event of a wet trip, I set up the tarp near the fire (taking care that sparks and flame won't burn it) or over the stove, for all to sit under while eating, reading, or playing quiet games.

Establish a well-defined kitchen area, toilet area, waste disposal bag, and sleeping area. Organization is the key to a successfully set-up camp. Food and cookware should be in one clearly designated area, while personal gear and what is needed for washing and cleaning up is in another. The backpacks should lean against a tree or rock, sheltered from rain, and near the tent. Once camp set-up is complete, you can kick back and enjoy the surroundings to their fullest.

THE WILDERNESS ETHIC

It is very important that you teach your children the ethics of the wilderness. Waste disposal, personal hygiene, cooking, cleaning, camp set-up, and camp break-down all have an effect on the surrounding environment. Your actions will determine whether your visit is a damaging one or goes relatively unnoticed.

When you set up the tent, pick an area that offers durable ground or duff, and not a grassy area that easily becomes matted down. Be sure there is good drainage away from the tent, so you will not have to play captain to a sinking ship in the middle of a downpour. It is never appropriate to dig drainage ditches around a tent. The ditches leave a permanent scar and rarely work as intended.

Open fires are becoming less and less acceptable as a means of warming and cooking. Stoves are kinder to the environment. Yet the romance of a crackling fire under a crisp, star-lit night sky is a wonderful experience. Let your conscience be your guide. If you choose to have a fire, however, there are some guidelines to keep in mind. Never break branches or twigs from a tree, even if they appear to be dead. To do so may cause the tree irreparable damage. When you collect wood for the fire, choose smaller branches and wood that will burn easily and completely in the fire. Go beyond the immediate area of the campsite to collect wood and never ever burn the last deadfall in the area—if wood seems sparse, use your stove.

When disposing human waste, use the cathole method. This involves digging a hole no more than 6 inches deep and at least 100 feet away from the nearest water source. Teach your children to defecate in the hole, but not to bury their toilet paper. Some outdoor experts say that toilet paper should be burned or carried out. Older, more responsible children, those who can safely handle matches, could be taught to burn the paper in the cat hole, making sure the fire is extinguished

You don't toss paper, wrappers, and food scraps on your living room carpet. Don't toss them away in the wilds, either. Pack out all that you pack in.

before leaving. I know of one group, camping in Baja California, who started a major fire because someone did not make sure that his toilet paper was extinguished.

If your family is going to stay in a base camp for a while, digging cat holes all around the area each time someone needs to go the toilet is not good practice. Instead, make a latrine or toilet area. Use a hole approximately 1 foot deep and 1 foot across. Leave a trowel by the hole so a small amount of soil can be sprinkled in the hole every time the latrine is used.

When washing dishes, brushing teeth, and washing your face and hands, do it over a sump hole dug 25 feet from camp and at least 100 feet from the nearest water source. The sump hole should drain well and not be any deeper than 6 inches. The idea behind the sump hole is to allow waste water to drain away and yet catch solid materials, such as food waste, for burning later or packing out.

When filling in a cat hole, latrine, or sump hole, use loose earth, pine needles, leaves, and twigs. Gently pack down the earth and try to match its appearance to that of the surrounding terrain.

If any waste cannot be burned, pack it out. Under no circumstances is it acceptable to bury human waste in the ground. Watch that younger children do not carelessly drop candy wrappers around the camp or on the trail. An excellent way to establish the proper tone is to set up a nylon trash sack immediately upon reaching your campsite. Then have everyone walk around and pick up any trash that is lying there before setting up anything. Demonstrate by word and example that wilderness must be kept clean for all to enjoy.

When breaking down camp, be sure to restore the area to its natural appearance as closely as possible. If you cleared sticks and twigs from an area under your tent, return them. Completely douse the fire with water and stir the mixture so the coals become cold to the touch. If there was an established fire ring at the campsite when you arrived, then leave it. If not, bury the coals, scatter the rocks, blackened side down, and smooth over the area. Walk through the camp with your children and make sure all signs of your visit are removed, and that all litter, yours or not, is carried out. Pack out all bite-sized and bigger bits of food that have collected in the sump hole and fill in the hole. Finally, fill in the latrine.

An excellent way to instill environmental concern in your children is to ask them to describe the site as it appears before you set up camp. Have them walk the chosen camp area with a notebook and write down what they observe. Then, when you are getting ready to leave, have them "supervise" and help you return the camp to its original appearance. The appearance of the camp area when you leave should be as good as—if not better than—it was originally. As you and they will find, there will always be an impact on the land, in the form of traffic lanes if nothing else. Perhaps this will help to foster a conviction that we must all take responsibility for our Earth.

Visiting Archaeological Sites

The single biggest problem for land managers and people managing cultural resources is dealing with damage—intentional and unintentional—caused by visitors. Even with extreme caution, damage does occur. It is imperative that you exercise extreme caution and respect when you visit archaeological and historic sites. Please teach your children wisely.

The following are rules that will guide you and your family through cultural sites with the least impact:

- View the site from a distance. Although there may be only one or two of you, there are literally thousands of the same groups of "one or two" visiting a site each year—that's a lot of foot traffic.
- Stop, look, and think before entering a cultural site. Identify the midden area (ancient trash pile) so you can avoid walking on it—middens contain important and fragile bits of archaeological information.
- Stay on any trail that has been built through a site.
- While looking at artifacts is fine, picking them up and taking them is not. Leave all potsherds and other artifacts where they lie, for others to enjoy.
- Camping is not allowed in or around ruins.
- Move nothing, not even branches or rocks, when you scramble around a site. Avoid touching plaster walls. Climbing on roofs and walls can lead to an immediate collapse of a cultural site that has stood for hundreds of years.
- Enjoy rock art by viewing, sketching, or photographing. Never chalk, trace, or otherwise touch rock art, as any kind of contact will cause the ancient figures to disintegrate.
- Creating graffiti is vandalism and a sacrilege.
- Never build fires in or around cultural sites.
- Finally, remember that cultural sites may be places of ancestral importance to Native Americans, and therefore demand treatment with the utmost respect and reverence.

Garlic and onion powder will save all but the most hopeless of culinary experiments outdoors.

Basic Cooking Tips

WORKING WITH FIRE OR STOVE

The fire or stove is the center of attention in every kitchen. A clear, 5-foot-diameter circle should be created around the cooking area. This area should be kept free of stray pieces of equipment, unneeded food, and wood. No running or playing should be permitted there. Always keep kitchen utensils in one place nearby, so that the cook will have easy access to them. Keep food and spices near the kitchen utensils so everything you need for the meal is close to hand.

Here are some very basic and mandatory rules to abide by when you are near a fire:

- Always wear shoes, as stray embers will burn your feet and can cause serious injury.
- Always remove pots from a fire when adding ingredients, to lessen the risk of burning yourself or wasting food. Use pot grabbers with work gloves to remove pots.
- A stray ember will melt nylon easily, so keep nylon clothing, tents, and sleeping gear away from the fire.
- Polypropylene, too, melts in very low heat. Getting too close to a fire while wearing polypropylene could create a painful burn if liner gloves or underwear melt on the skin—I have melted a pair of gloves on one hand myself and it hurt.
- Never, ever leave a fire unattended—if you leave for any reason, put it out.
- Remember that having a fire is a privilege and not a right. If the area appears overcamped and wood is scarce, or if build-

Wooden bowls keep hot food warmer longer and seem more natural in a wilderness setting than do metal and plastic ones.

ing a fire would permanently scar the land (for example, land near or above the timberline), then opt for a stove.

Although you must be very careful with children around open flames, it is important to involve them with the building and maintaining of fires. It is crucially important for them to realize that building fires is serious business and not play. If they cannot take fire-building seriously and are apt to play around with flaming sticks, you should take away their fire-helping privileges.

Although children of all ages make excellent wood gatherers, generally it is not until they reach the ages of 10 or 11 that they become patient and responsible enough to be trusted with the task of building fires. At this age, they are able to build a fire carefully, using kindling, smaller twigs, and then larger sticks to feed the growing flame. By the ages of 10 or 11, they seem to have developed sufficient maturity to respect the power of flame, particularly if parents have set the proper example.

COOKING IN CAMP

The first and perhaps most important rule is never to cook too much food. Try to judge your food needs with precision. If you end up with extra food in the pan after a meal, you must not bury it because that would attract bugs, rodents, and other animals that wouldn't ordinarily visit the campsite. Besides, humans' food rarely does an animal any good, and in

When walking, choose a mountaineer's pace—a slow, methodical, inexorable, and relatively rhythmical step that can be maintained all day long without creating sweat or exhaustion.

many cases does it harm. If you have a fire, burn the extra food. Otherwise, pack it out—no exceptions.

Almost anything that is prepared at home can be prepared outdoors. A backpacking stove or the glowing coals of a fire are similar in function, if not appearance, to an oven range at home. Temperatures can be controlled. Always cook on low flames with a stove, and on hot coals with no flame on a fire. Choose a cooking site protected from the wind.

When building a fire, it is best to use wood that is no bigger around than your thumb. This will help to create an excellent bed of coals fairly rapidly. Finger-sized wood will burn almost completely and will be much easier to clean up and dispose of afterward than larger branches that do not burn through completely. While you are cooking, keep a small fire going at one end of the pit and periodically rake the hot embers toward the pots.

BAKING OUTDOORS

There are many backpacking ovens designed to let you bake outdoors. Inspect them at your local outdoor-gear store.

Establish clear and mandatory rules dealing with fires.

There are even ready-made mixes for creating delicious brownies, quiches, coffee cakes, pizza and more. Although most camping ovens break down for easy transport, you still have to bear their weight, of course. Still, I don't know of any child who wouldn't be thrilled at the thought of brownies when camping.

If you don't want to buy a proprietary oven, you can still bake on a backpacking stove or over a fire, but it will take some ingenuity and patience on your part. The idea is to create a type of Dutch oven using a frying pan and a lid. You can use the low flame of a stove to heat the bottom of the "oven," and a small twig fire burning on the lid to heat the upper part. But I have had more consistent success with an open fire. The temperature of the fire is critical. If your hand, held about 6 inches from the bed of embers, feels hot but not uncomfortable, then the fire is ready. Be sure you have a very good supply of hot coals. Place the frying pan on a level bed of embers and then shovel a generous layer on top of the lid. You will need to check the baking periodically. Brush off the top coals and quickly look inside without letting in cold air. Always keep flames away from the frying pan.

Children will have fun baking Bisquick horns if you can stand the mess. Mix 6 parts of Bisquick mix to 1 part water. Knead the dough until it is firm and not too sticky. Divide the dough into equal parts and then roll each part into long snakes. Find fairly sturdy sticks about 3 feet long (don't ever cut green wood for this) and whittle a smooth, 6-inch surface on one end. Wrap the dough snakes around the smooth ends of each stick tightly and bake over hot coals (not flames) until

Keeping your sleeping bag dry is essential for safety and comfort.

golden brown. When they are done, the horns should easily slide off each stick, leaving a steaming pastry just waiting to be filled with jam or honey.

HELPFUL HINTS

- Powdered and instant mixes do not dissolve well in cold water and sometimes not even in boiling water. If you make a paste first by mixing 1 part of the mix with 1 part of warm water, you'll have fewer lumps.
- For thickening, use 1 part water to 1 part flour, Cream of Rice, or instant potatoes.
- Cheese tends to become clumped or stringy when you add it directly to dishes with a watery base, such as stews or soups. It is better to melt the cheese first and then add it to the dish.
- Remember that cooking at altitude will take longer because water boils there before it reaches 212°F. Additionally, wind and cold temperatures will draw heat away from the stove, so it is important to use a good wind screen and cook in the best shelter possible.
- Burned food can be prevented by cooking on low heat, in clean pots, with frequent stirring.
- Bland food is very often due to a lack of salt or other spices, but most usually salt. Salt can easily be overdone, especially if the ingredients you are using are salty themselves, but a pinch of salt or salt substitute does tend to bring out the flavor in foods.
- Undercooking or overcooking is usually caused by adding ingredients in the wrong order, or by poor timing. Always add freeze-dried foods first before adding additional rice or pasta. If you are adding thickeners, milk, or cheese to the dish, add

Always let someone know where you are going and when you will be back—and let them know when you have returned.

them just before the dish is done. If you add them too soon they will burn or stick to the bottom of the pan.

CLEANING UP

Keep pots and utensils clean. Use hot water to wash pots and utensils after each use. Don't leave them lying around dirty. Instead of using a plastic scrubby or Brillo pad, which quickly become breeding grounds for bacteria, try a handful of coarse grass, sand, pine cones, or pine needles. Use boiling water to sterilize your dishes and pots. Sterilize your cooking utensils in a small amount of boiling water before using them each evening. Save the water for clean-up chores after the meal. Avoid using too much camp soap because it is very hard to rinse off and may leave a film that can lead to diarrhea.

If food sticks to the bottom of a pan, add boiling water to the pan and let it sit overnight. This usually softens the burned-on food sufficiently for proper cleaning in the morning. Always wash dishes at least 100 feet away from the nearest water source. Dump rinse water and tiny food particles into a sump hole under a bush and away from camp.

One of the most obvious ways to stay healthy is to wash your hands. Buck Tilton, co-author of *Camping Healthy, Hygiene for the Outdoors* (Globe Pequot), advises washing the hands after bowel movements, before attending to wounds, and always before preparing food. It is estimated that between 25 and 40 percent of all foodborne illness is transmitted by unwashed hands.

Water between 100°F and 120°F, almost too hot to touch, is best at cleaning hands, but does not remove all the bacteria. Soap up, and work the lather into the skin and under the nails for at least 30 seconds. Rinse thoroughly with hot water again. Re-soap, re-rinse and then dry. Drying is perhaps one of the most overlooked and yet most important steps, since washing alone will leave some bacteria suspended in the droplets of water clinging to your skin, enhancing the possibility of a chance migration from skin to food.

Of course, in the backcountry, hot water is a rare thing indeed, unless you are packing copious volumes of fuel. For wilderness use when hot water becomes a luxury, Tilton recommends the use of a germicidal soap such as Betadine Scrub, Hibiclens, or Klenz-Blu Gel.

"Sure, washing your hands so meticulously is a bother, but so is getting sick," says Tilton. "Remember most of all, however, that even plain old unscientific hand washing beats no hand washing at all."

Here are some more hygiene tips from Tilton:

- Do not share bandannas, toothbrushes, razors, water bottles, eating utensils, and so on.
- Wash and air-dry all community kitchen gear.
- Keep anyone who is ill, or appears to be ill, out of the kitchen area.
- Purify all drinking water by filtration, chemical treatment, or boiling.

Dealing with Wild Animals

Before going camping you should find out what animals may frequent your campsite. From kangaroo rats to bears, animals are an inquisitive lot and are likely to take any food they can get hold of. A kangaroo rat gnawing through a pack to get at some nuts inside is not a physical threat to you, but the damage to the pack could create real problems.

Don't dry a pair of boots in front of a fire, unless you are planning to eat them.

A bear, on the other hand, rummaging through camp and smelling food in a tent is going to be very surprised when it encounters humans as well as chocolate or fish. The surprise and resulting screaming and growling can lead to very unfortunate reactions. In a conflict between a bear and an unarmed human, the bear always comes off best.

If you are going to camp in areas such as the Great Smoky Mountains of Tennessee, Yellowstone National Park in Montana, or Yosemite National Park in California, learn to bear-proof things. To minimize the chances of a surprise encounter with a bear, hang food well away from camp, leave no food in packs, and never ever take into tents any food, or clothes that smell of food.

No matter what part of the nation you camp in, you need to animal-proof your gear. If there is no bear hazard, and you choose not to hang your food, I would recommend that at the very least you leave pack pockets open and do not take food into the tent. An eager rodent will gnaw through fabric to get to food, but will usually take the easy route if you leave a zipper or flap open.

Campsite Chores

Every camping trip is going to involve its own set of chores and demands such as setting up camp, breaking down camp, laying out sleeping bags, stuffing sleeping bags, cooking, cleaning, hanging food, and so on. Though it may seem easier to do everything yourself, children must be encouraged to do their

Although cotton is lousy in cold weather, loose-fitting cotton clothing is great for desert travel.

share of chores. In reality, you won't save any time or effort while you are directing young children's labor, but setting the precedent of requiring a child to help with tasks now is important if you wish them to be of assistance as they get older.

Use the extra set of little hands to help you roll out the tent, separate the stakes, assemble the poles, even hold up an end of the tent while you secure the other. Give your child the task of unpacking everyone's sleeping pads and bags and laying them out neatly in the tent. It may take an incredibly long time, but children seem universally to enjoy this activity and it is well within their capabilities.

During cooking time, young children should not be playing around the fire or stove. Nevertheless, children love to help with cooking by adding water and mixing ingredients. This can easily be accomplished if you set up an area away from the fire and the main food preparation area to reduce the amount of dirt kicked in food and the number of pots knocked over. It is important for your children to realize that when they are given a cooking task, they need to sit still under adult supervision until the task is done and then they must move completely away from the cooking area until the food is served.

Younger children often enjoy playing in warm dishwater. You can capitalize on this desire by giving them cups and utensils to clean (no knives) after most of the other pots and pans have been cleaned. Chances are they will enjoy playing and cleaning in the water for quite some time.

Exercise caution in assigning chores. If a child has had a long hot day on the trail and is exhausted, it might be best to let him or her rest rather than help with the cooking or setting up of the tent.

As your children get older, they can take on more difficult chores and participate in the day-to-day activities of the camp. In all situations, try to create a positive atmosphere and work with your children. The only time I have seen a child show a really negative response to chores was when a parent sat on his duff and assigned all the work, never once lifting a finger himself. All aspects of wilderness travel must involve teamwork to be successful.

Other Campsite Activities

There are an infinite number of activities that will interest you and your children around camp. Chapter 5 details specific projects that teach observation skills and nature awareness. As with any activity you choose, be sure that it always follows these guidelines: It must be safe. It must not disturb the wildlife. It must not damage the environment in any way. And it should be fun.

Singing around the campfire is a time-honored tradition. If, like me, you have trouble remembering songs I would suggest you get hold of the book *Campfire Songs,* edited by Irene Maddox and Rosalyn Blankenship (Globe Pequot). It's filled with rounds, songs, and ballads, many with guitar chords.

Stargazing is great fun and an informative activity. Unless you can conjure up stories of legend and tales of bravery to go with the galactic formations, however, looking at stars is best reserved for older children. Many stores sell compact star guides that will help you identify those bright twinkles in the sky.

Tree climbing, crawfish hunting, firefly chasing, cloud watching, meadow crawling, hide and seek, and many other games flit through the minds of youngsters. No game will hold interest long, of course, but with a little help the hours should pass with never a dull moment for anyone.

Tips in a Nutshell

1. Be creative, use games, keep patient—variety and perseverance will get your family through a hike successfully.
2. Take frequent rest breaks—every 30 minutes is average. Be sure that you and your children snack, drink, and rest at every scheduled stop.
3. Don't use food as a motivational tool except in a real emergency. Once at camp, establish firm camp boundaries immediately. Children are not to go beyond those boundaries without a parent present.
4. Establish well-defined kitchen, toilet, garbage, and sleeping areas.
5. Teach your children to be environmentally responsible. Waste disposal, personal hygiene, cooking, cleaning, fires, and playing all have a lasting impact on your surroundings.
6. Always animal-proof your gear, your tent, and your camp.
7. Encourage children to do their share of chores. Small children may need your help, but you will be setting a precedent that will encourage participation as they get older.

 CHAPTER 5

Learning About Nature

THERE IS A TREMENDOUS AMOUNT IN NATURE FOR YOU AND your children to discover together. Yet, as inquisitive as children naturally are, they will learn much more with your encouragement and example. Your family needn't become entomologists, botanists, or ecologists to appreciate what nature has to offer, but there are some activities and techniques that will help to make each trip outdoors more meaningful.

In this chapter you will learn how to use your senses, all of them, to make the most out of discovery. Your senses will show you and your children how to become truly one with the wilderness. Learned individuals have already carefully documented and named most of the plants, insects, and animals you will encounter, but what is more important for you is to know something for what it truly is, and not just by its name. Young children really aren't impressed by knowing that they are looking at an acorn woodpecker. They are more interested in its shape, its size, the sounds it makes, how it flies, and its color. Older children, however, realize that knowing a bird's name will enable them to learn more about it from reference sources, so they will enjoy looking up the name in a guidebook.

Your job as a parent will be to see things as a child does. Learn to look beyond the name and view things with curios-

Try to see things as a child would. An insect's scientific name is not as important as, say, its size or color.

ity and sensitivity. If you can do this and become really aware of natural things, you will enter a child's world of thrills and experiences. Is there any better way to relate to your children than that? A coyote's yelp under a moonlit sky, the dart of a mouse scampering among leaves, the sweet aroma of a dew-laden meadow under the morning sun, the iridescence of a trout as it swims in the shallows of a mountain brook—all these wonderful moments will be missed if you are unobservant.

Taking time to smell the roses, keeping your eyes and ears open, and thrilling to every discovery will make all of you acutely aware of your surroundings. In the truest meaning of the term, you and your family will become amateur naturalists.

To put together a "discovery kit" for your children you will need a small nylon stuffsack containing the following items: a handheld magnifying glass; several bandannas; several small, unbreakable, clear plastic specimen containers; an aquarium net; a small notebook and pencil; a set of colored pencils; and several sheets of tracing paper. If you wish, you can make an underwater viewer using a large coffee can with both ends cut out. Over one end, stretch clear plastic wrap and secure it in place with a rubber band. Now, when you place the plastic-covered end into the water, you will be able to see under water in a stream or pond.

The most important concept for your children to learn is never to remove anything from its natural environment. With an adult's supervision, it is okay to pick up and examine a small bug, or lizard, or even a frog or two, but keep skin contact to a minimum and always return the critters to where you found them. This is where the clear plastic specimen containers come in handy. When you are examining a bug or small lizard up close, gently place it in the container and then look at it through the magnifying glass. This will help reduce the stress of being held in a human hand for any length of time. Always keep captivity to a minimum—longer than one minute is pushing it. If your children learn respect for each and every creature in the wilderness, they will have learned one of the most important lessons of all.

Your Own Backyard

The backyard is an excellent place in which to begin to teach children more about plants and animals. Building bird feeders and creating a wild garden in one corner of the yard are both excellent ways to bring a wilderness feel to an urban environment.

> The perfect campsite is discovered, never created.

When crossing streams, wear a pair of all-terrain sandals. Don't go barefoot, as you risk injury. Don't wear your boots, as you risk blisters and foot discomfort if you hike in wet footgear.

Bird feeders are more than elaborate trays or concrete dishes filled with seed. To attract a wide variety of birds, you need a wide variety of feeders. Hummingbird feeding tubes filled with red sugar water, several dishes of seed near dense bushes on the ground, and perhaps one or two feeding platforms elevated on 4 × 4s, offer an excellent blend. Don't forget to give them water as well. The ideal backyard includes dense bushes and shrubbery for birds to perch in after and during feeding. Birds seem to feel more protected and secure this way and are more apt to frequent your yard and perhaps nest there as well. Once you begin feeding the birds, don't stop. They will become dependent upon the feed you and your child are providing and could starve if you suddenly quit putting seed in the feeding stations.

If at all possible, put the feeders close to a window. This will allow you and your children to observe birds without disturbing them. Keep a pair of binoculars and an identification book near the window.

If you use your imagination, you can create a wild garden that doesn't violate any city ordinances. With the addition of a few rocks, perhaps a small artificial pond, and some carefully selected wildflowers and plants, a corner of your yard can be turned into a mini-wilderness that many forms of wildlife will find attractive.

Improving children's observation skills and heightening their awareness is important. Show them that they have more than eyes with which to "see" the environment. It is through their initial experiences in a backyard or park that your children will come to realize that nature is all around them—under the blades of grass, behind the pile of bricks in the corner of the yard, in the branches overhead, and in the eaves of the garage.

Watching Wildlife

Here are some things to help you enjoy watching wildlife:

- Keep your distance. You can harm wildlife unintentionally by getting too close. Most wild animals react with alarm when humans approach on foot. A panic reaction is stressful and causes the animal to use up energy and food reserves. Repeated disturbances can cause animals and birds to avoid an area, even when it offers the best food and habitat. Learn to identify animal behavior that will warn you if you are getting too close. Be advised that you will get your closest peeks at wildlife if you keep your distance and allow them to come to you. Never use food to attract animals.
- Use spotting equipment. Quality binoculars with a minimum of seven magnifications and 35-mm front lenses (7 × 35) or a spotting scope will help you to observe wildlife from a safe distance. Use a telephoto lens (300 mm) and tripod to get close-up photos.
- Take your time. Rushing around is no way to watch wildlife. It is important that you show your children that the more time you take, the greater your chances of observing wildlife that would otherwise be missed. Set up a base camp and spend a few days in a given area. You are most likely to spot wild animals at or around dawn and dusk.
- Blend in. Wear muted colors, sit quietly and leave pets at home. Refrain from using scented soaps or perfumes. Sitting quietly is often the hardest thing a child has to learn. Consequently, I would advise you not to spend too much time sit-

With a little care—and caution—there's no telling what you might encounter.

ting and waiting because the only thing you will teach your children is that wildlife watching is bor-r-r-ing!

- Research. Spend time at local museums of natural history to learn about the wildlife in the area you are visiting. Natural history museums and organizations have books, brochures, maps and displays that will help you. Learn to recognize an animal by its tracks, droppings, and sounds.
- Carry field guides. Many field guides concentrate on specific areas, describing their birds, mammals, animal tracks, edible plants, wildflowers, trees, rocks and gems, and so on. Most major bookstores should carry a selection. There are also many field guides written for young people, giving your children a chance to learn alongside you.
- Keep your distance. You are too close to a bird if it seems skittish, raises its head to watch you, preens excessively, pecks at dirt or its feet, wipes its bill repeatedly, gives alarm calls, flushes repeatedly, or tries to distract you by feigning a broken wing or some other injury. In other words, if it seems agitated.

- Keep your distance. You are too close to a mammal if it raises its head high, points its ears in your direction, raises hairs on its neck and shoulders, exhibits signs of skittishness (such as jumping at sounds or movements), lowers its head, puts it ears back in preparation for a charge, moves away, or displays aggressive or nervous behavior.

Special Backyard Games

Here are some games you and your children can play in your own backyard to foster an interest in nature and the outdoors.

BACKYARD CRAWL. The object of the backyard crawl is to teach your children to move slowly and alertly through their environment. Show them how to peer into branches, pull back blades of grass, and examine an overturned stone. Every move should be methodical. Children should be encouraged to scan all around them while they crawl across the yard, looking repeatedly from side to side, above, below, and behind—just like an animal trying to stay alert to danger and food.

LIMITED VISION. The object of this exercise is to show children what it is like to see the world through the eyes of different animals. You can do this quite simply by cutting toilet paper tubes in half and then taping them to an old pair of sunglasses. Place tape on the glasses to block all vision except through each eye tube. Then have your children walk around discovering a new perspective of their backyard. If you wish to get more technical, lenses are available from the Nature Company of Berkeley, California, that offer your child a look at the world through compound eyes like a bug's. Either system obscures vision and should be used only under adult supervision and in a relatively clear area free of dangerous obstacles.

OBSERVATION PLOT. With your child, mark off a 2-foot by 2-foot square in a section of the yard. Put stakes in each corner and fasten string to each stake to create a permanent, definable boundary. This little square is your child's to watch and observe from day to day and season to season. Have him or her keep a little notebook of what is observed. What happens to the plants? What kind of insects or animals live there? What animals or insects just pass through? What is the earth like? How much sun does the area get? How much rain? How do the sun and rain affect the area? The list of questions is almost endless and the involvement of your child in the area is limited only by his or her curiosity and your encouragement.

NIGHT VIGIL. Walking at night with your children in the wilderness is an experience not to be missed. It can however, be a somewhat frightening experience for first timers, so it is best enjoyed after a little forethought and preparation. You can prepare in your own backyard.

Pick a clear, moonless night. Turn out all the lights in the house so there is a minimum of artificial light illuminating the backyard. With a flashlight, walk out into the backyard and sit down under a tree or somewhere comfortable. Bring a blanket along if you wish. Turn the flashlight on and show your child that although it seems lighter with the flashlight, your vision is really limited to the beam of the light. Now, turn off the light and sit quietly. Explain and talk about each sound as you hear it—a dog barking, a bat flitting through the air, a

In bear country, never bring food into a tent, never sleep in clothing that smells of freshly caught fish, always hang your food away from camp, and always yield right of way to a bear.

siren, a mouse rustling in the compost pile. Begin to help your child distinguish between sounds that are heard in the day and those heard at night. Ask him or her why some animals come out only at night and what makes them different from daytime animals? How does the backyard seem different in the dark? Why? When the time seems right, walk back to the house without the flashlight. Point out to your child how much better your vision is overall without the light.

Head for the Woods

Here are some mind-expanding games and exercises you and your children can enjoy in local parks or nature preserves, depending on what they have to offer:

HUG A TREE. This is an excellent exercise that teaches children to really begin tapping into their perceptual skills. Blindfold your child and lead him or her to a nearby tree. Have your child get to really know the tree by hugging it, touching it, smelling it, tasting it, listening to it. Ask him or her to describe the tree to you—its size, its age, its shape. Once your child feels that she really knows the tree, lead her away, spin her around and remove the blindfold. Now ask her to find her tree.

Children will discover that it requires all their senses to do this and that it is possible to "see" and "know" an object without using your eyes. Be a participant in this one, too—let your child blindfold you and lead you through the exercise.

STREAM WALK. Playing in a stream is one of my favorite exercises. Be sure that everyone is wearing old tennis shoes and that the day is warm. Beware of slippery rocks, sharp sticks and other objects, poisonous snakes, and hypothermia. If the water is cold, do not stay in too long. Bring along magnifying glasses, aquarium nets, and several face masks or clear plastic dishes about 6 inches across. You may also use your homemade underwater viewing can. Pick a section of stream through your local park that is not too difficult to navigate, not too long, and not too deep. The idea is to wade down the middle of the stream slowly and methodically. Look for minnows, frogs, tadpoles, crawfish, and so on. Use the net to scoop up animals and look at them in the dishes. Use your masks or place the dishes in the water for a glass-window view of the stream below the surface. Romp, play, and get dirty. Wallow in mud holes; explore every nook and cranny. If you come upon a still pool, have your children stand quietly observing the world below them through masks or the glass dishes floating on the surface. If they are able to stand still for longer than a minute, they will get a peek at another world swimming around their legs.

SWAMP MUCKING. This is a variation on the stream walk with one major difference—you get really muddy. Talk about immersing yourself in nature! When I led groups into the swamp at camp, squeals of happiness and curiosity overcame the nervous apprehension of things slimy and gross. Interestingly, parents who had heard about it from their children's letters home inquired if they, too, could go swamp mucking. The idea is to crawl through the swamp following open waterways and animal paths. Use obvious caution before diving into a swamp that might be home to alligators, water moccasins, leeches, or snapping turtles.

> Cultural sites are places of ancestral importance to Native Americans and demand to be treated with the respect and reverence they deserve. Look but don't touch or collect.

FOX AND HARE. This is a fun game that will go a long way in teaching your children to become aware of their surroundings, so they are able to follow the trail of something from the signs it leaves. Begin by designating the hare, usually a parent, and the foxes, usually the children, and another parent for supervision. Initially, the hare should get a 2-minute to 5-minute start—sufficient for the foxes to lose sight of the hare. The hare will leave signs for the foxes to follow, such as bits of colored paper on the ground or in branches—not too obvious, yet distinct enough to be followed with minimal effort. As the children gain experience, the hare should get a longer headstart and should begin leaving bits of paper that more closely match the color of the terrain. As a variation, the hare can drag a branch behind him, leaving a more subtle trail for the foxes to follow. The object of the game is for the foxes to follow the trail of the hare and catch him. Use your imagination to adapt the game to local conditions.

BLIND TRUST. This will teach your child to listen carefully to directions as well as learning to utilize other senses of awareness. It will also teach your child important communication and leadership skills. You will want to play this game in a fairly wooded area with some small hills and narrow gullies or other obstacles. Blindfold all in the group except the designated leader. First time around, the designated leader should be an adult. The idea is for the leader to guide his or her group through the woods going over, around, and under obstacles using only voice commands to give directions. At no time is the leader allowed to move obstacles or touch the players. I would recommend that at all times a parent or other adult keep a watchful eye on the group to maintain a margin of safety. I once had a child try to lead his group over a gully using a narrow log as a bridge. The 10-foot fall that could have resulted was not my idea of the best way to learn.

Small rodents can smell food in a pack and will chew through your pack fabric—leave all your pack pockets open.

SNAPSHOT OPPORTUNITY. This game is great fun and can be played anywhere. It will teach children to be efficient and accurate observers. The idea is for one person to be the camera or lens, and the other person to work the shutter. One person should guide the "camera" in search of a good photograph—a beautiful, interesting, or creative image that the camera can take a picture of. The camera, meanwhile, must keep his or her eyes closed. The guide should then set up the camera in front of the chosen picture, which is taken by tapping the camera on the shoulder or hand. The camera opens his or her eyes without moving or twisting about and stares at the image in front. After about five seconds, the guide taps on the shoulder or hand of the camera and the camera's eyes close again. Allow your child to be the "photographer," using you as the camera, and you will be afforded a unique and quite possibly very moving look at what your child considers fascinating and beautiful.

BAREFOOT IN THE WOODS. Going barefoot is a most natural experience, yet one that is rarely enjoyed. To go barefoot encourages one to slow down, feel the ground underfoot, and relive an almost primeval instinct. Be sure that the ground you are going to walk over is relatively free of sharp rocks, thorns, and yes, even glass. Lead your youngsters through the woods in single file. Teach them to stalk, that is, to walk as if hunting, through the trees. To do this, take a very small and very careful step forward to the outside ball of your descending foot. Very slowly, and without placing any weight on it, roll the foot to the inside of the ball. If you don't feel anything underfoot that may break with a loud snap or pop, carefully lower your heel and then place your full weight on the foot. If your child becomes adept at this, he or she will be able to sneak up to birds and animals without spooking them. The key is slow and steady movements.

PRACTICE STALKING. Have one person, the prey, sit with his or her eyes closed at one end of a clearing about 25 feet wide. Everyone else tries to stalk the prey without being heard. If the prey hears a sound he or she points to it and opens his or her eyes. If the stalker is able to freeze and not move while the prey is watching, the game continues. If, however, the stalker moves at all, even a flinch, the stalker becomes the prey.

WORLD ABOVE AND WORLD BELOW. This activity is a quiet observational game that will work only if your children are feeling calm and not overly agitated. This game can be played anywhere and is limited only by imagination. To study the world above, everyone must lie still and quietly on their backs, looking up at the world above. I find it is most effective to play this game under a dense canopy of leaves or swirling clouds, or in dense, tall grass.

Looking down takes place with everyone on their stomachs. They watch the world as it passes by their faces. Looking down works outstandingly well at the edge of a stream or lake, or above a tide pool, a dense patch of grasses, or fallen leaves. I have found it helpful, if the ground is cold or hard, to bring sleeping pads for everyone.

Tidepooling

Exploring tidepools, especially with a young child or an older adult who is young at heart, is an absolute hoot. Poking and peering into pools searching for crabs, sea urchins, sea shells,

Given a choice, camp in the most impacted site rather than spread the impact to a less-visited area.

Never bury food scraps. They will get dug up and scattered.

sea cucumbers, octopus, starfish, and the like can keep you and your kids occupied and entertained for hours. I've whiled away many an afternoon meandering from pool to pool or walking along northwestern beaches during low spring tides, searching out what was previously untouchable.

To make the trip more enjoyable, I would recommend taking along a viewing "eye." I use an old diving mask that, when pressed up against my face and then placed into the water, allows me to see underwater. As we've already discussed, you can also make a viewer by cutting the bottom out of an old #10 coffee can and then covering the can opening with clear plastic wrap secured with a rubber band. Just place the can into the water, plastic end down, and you'll be amazed how clearly you can see. Sometimes, you may wish to turn over a rock or log to see what lives under it. Do so carefully and gently, taking care not to crush what lives underneath. Replace the rock with equal care when you have finished looking. Never turn your back on the ocean, or you risk getting drenched by a sneaky wave. Please don't collect from the beach anything that is still alive. In most cases it is illegal, but apart from that, marine animals are much better off in a wild environment. Finally, remember as you wander that beaches (or uplands) and their tidelands (those parts of a beach that are alternately covered and uncovered by rising and falling tides) may be privately owned in some states. They may not, however, be signposted as private. It is your responsibility to know whether or not you are treading on public or private land. If in doubt, ask at the public access point before venturing out.

Stargazing

Stargazing with children is a wonderful experience, made even more special by being able to "discover" stars and constellations together. For most city-trapped youngsters, the sight of thousands of pinpricks of light twinkling against the inky-black backdrop of a night sky is a new experience. It's easy to forget that the lights of a city mask the stars, leaving children no chance to see the world beyond earth unless they step away from the city and gaze skyward from a mountaintop or an open field. Stargazing takes practice and patience, but with a "star wheel" (available at most nature, outdoor, or hobby stores) and a star guide you'll open up an awe-inspiring new world. Here is a brief list of favorite and easily found stars and constellations visible in the Northern Hemisphere:

- The North Star, or Polaris. The beauty of the North Star is that it stays in one place in the sky, always to the north of you. To pick it out of the mass of other twinkling stars, find the Big Dipper (otherwise known as the Great Bear or the Plow) and locate the two stars that make up the outer edge of the dipper's ladle. A straight line joining the two, extended five times, will reach the North Star.

> Hats are more than fashion statements. They serve the function of keeping the head shaded, the face shielded, the brain cool, and all the time providing a place to hang your favorite flies for fishing.

- Cassiopeia. This constellation was named for the mythological wife of King Cepheus, of Ethiopia. Look for a five-star cluster shaped like a "W" or an "M" near the north or northeast horizon just before midnight in a summer sky.
- Ursa Major. This is the Great Bear, of which the Big Dipper is a part. The Dipper makes up the Bear's back, and the handle is the Bear's nose. Three pairs of stars make up the Bear's paws.
- Bootes. This constellation, also known as The Herdsman, includes Arcturus, the fourth brightest star in the sky. Arcturus takes on a distinct orange color and sits at the constellation's base. The Herdsman resembles a large kite.
- Leo. The Lion lies just below the Bear's paws, between the Great Bear and the western horizon. The bluish-white star Regulus sits near the Lion's chest and behind its front leg.

Tips in a Nutshell

1. Become more concerned with shape, size, color, texture, sound, smell, and taste than with the correct scientific name.
2. Learn to view everything for the first time, as if through the eyes of a child.
3. Assemble a discovery kit for your children.
4. Never remove anything from the natural environment, and always handle animals minimally and carefully.
5. Turn your backyard into an urban wilderness by making a wash-basin pond, a wild garden, and several bird feeding stations.

CHAPTER 6

Family Fun in the Snow

CROSS-COUNTRY SKIING, OR NORDIC SKI TOURING, IS GREAT fun with children, provided you have some shelter from the cold. The site should be easily accessible and the terrain not too difficult. Choosing a cabin for a base, with surrounding meadows laden in snow, is good. Choosing a resort with set tracks, teaching areas, warming huts along the trail, certified instructors, a children's teaching program, and lots of other activities, is even better.

Modern snowshoes enable you and your children to hike and even run in wilderness snow. You can cover a lot of ground this way, even more than you would on cross-country skis, and visit a lot of sites otherwise inaccessible in winter. And once you have snowshoes, no other special gear is required. Wear standard hiking boots and dress in layers, as you would for normal hiking, and you're all set.

Let's take a look at each activity in turn:

Cross-Country Skiing

The skills necessary to stay on your feet and have fun on cross-country skis are quite easily acquired. More and more ski resorts have excellent teaching programs for families and children. I

Take time out for a rest break for five to ten minutes each hour. If it is chilly, seek out sunny and wind-protected locations.

would heartily recommend that everyone in your family who doesn't know how to cross-country ski take a lesson from a professional. Learning from a family member or close friend can be rewarding, but more often than not this experience ends in frustration for all. What is so wonderful about Nordic skiing is that everyone can do it, and by teaching your family you are giving your children a skill they can use all their lives.

EQUIPMENT

Equipment for cross-country skiing, while still far cheaper than that for downhill skiing, is increasing in price. You should, however, still be able to purchase waxless skis, a good pair of boots, bindings, and poles for under $250 for adults, and under $100 for children. Spend some time shopping

Nordic skiing will open the door to an incredible number of adventures—and it's easy to learn and relatively inexpensive.

around. Do not just buy the cheapest—you get what you pay for in this sport. Karhu and Fischer make special children's skis and ski packages. Give them a good inspection.

Always buy waxless skis for children. On the average, standard cross-country skis should be about a child's height for children 5 years or younger. Children aged 6 years and older can begin to ski with longer skis—up to 8 inches (20 centimeters) longer than his or her height, on average.

When in doubt, buy skis that are short rather than long because your children will initially be more concerned with gripping than gliding. Longer skis glide more easily but have less grip; conversely, shorter skis offer great grip, but reduced glide. A child who cannot climb a hill or push around on a gentle grade without slipping backward and falling down is a frustrated child who will quickly decide skiing is a waste of time. A number of years ago, a new "shorty ski" was designed. I prefer it for children. The first was a ski by Fischer called the Revolution. Now, every major cross-country ski company offers this type of ski. The advantage is that they turn more easily, are easier to put on, are easier to play in and are more versatile.

Boots for younger children, 3 to 5 years of age, should be the same warm and waterproof type they wear to play in the snow. These boots can be attached to the ski with a simple strap or cable binding. For school-age children, use a boot and binding system that they can easily manage on their own. Salomon Nordic System (SNS) and New Nordic Norm (NNN) boot and binding systems are easily handled by small fingers, yet they still offer plenty of support for more adventurous

During rest breaks in the cold, put on extra insulation and sit on a foam pad, not directly on cold ground, which can suck the heat and life right out of you.

Just because a manufacturer says a sleeping bag will keep you warm at 20°F doesn't make it so.

When winter camping, save the toilet paper and use snow, but watch out for those ice crystals—ouch!

skiers. Avoid buying boots that need to be grown into. Instead, take advantage of the many ski boot trade-in programs offered by retailers around the nation.

Poles are best avoided for children under the age of 5 years, but older children will want and probably need poles. Poles should be shorter, in proportion to height, than the adult sizes. Until the child successfully learns to use his or her poles, have the sharp metal tips blunted to avoid possible injuries and accidents.

Pulka sleds are ideal for the family with children too young to ski, but who want to go skiing with the family anyway. It is not safe to carry infants and toddlers in backpacks or child carriers on ski tours. Children's legs can get constricted in a pack or child carrier, which can lead to frostbite, and the reduced circulation can promote hypothermia. The pulka is made of wood or fiberglass and is designed to carry as many as three children and/or supplies. The sled is remarkably easy to control since it's towed behind an adult who is wearing a padded waist or shoulder harness. A waterproof cover will keep the tiny passengers dry and protected from the wind.

CLOTHING

If children are cold, they are miserable. Layers of clothes are far better for them than are single bulky garments. When choosing what to buy, the guidelines are primarily the same as mentioned in Chapter 2 on buying clothing. Remember that if the child is being towed in a pulka, he or she is not generating any warmth through exercising, and extra care must be taken to maintain his or her body temperature. You will develop a sense about when to adjust the layers of clothing, depending on a child's mood; often he or she will get grumpy instead of saying "I'm too hot."

Create an inner layer consisting of polypropylene, silk, Thermax, Polartec, or Capilene; several outer layers of fleece, Polartec, bunting, or wool (although I prefer to stay away from wool because it is scratchy and often provides one more thing for the child to worry about); and a windproof, waterproof, breathable outer layer. Above all, avoid cotton—it does nothing but absorb water and freeze.

For the outer layer, I recommend a separate top and bottom shell—the rain suit top and bottom that you purchased for backpacking is an ideal choice. The exception would be children between the ages of 3 and 5. For them you will want a one-piece suit with a hood attached. They do fall down a lot and the one-piece suit will prevent snow from falling down their necks and creeping up their backs.

Hats and mittens are critical. The hat should be made from wool with a non-itch lining, or from bunting. Mittens are better than gloves for keeping tiny hands warm but should not be too bulky, otherwise it will be difficult for them to grip poles, snowballs, and their playmates. Buy mittens with a waterproof shell, a removable one if it's available. If children are quick to pull off the mittens, pin or clip them to the sleeve of the snowsuit or jacket.

TEACHING

If you are going to teach your children to ski, or as you follow up on skills taught in a professional lesson, go easy. Don't attempt to turn your children into skiing professionals the first day. Pick a meadow with a gently rolling area and lots of room

> When it comes to socks, more is not necessarily warmer. Your feet must have room in your boots, otherwise they will become constricted and freeze.

to play and stay together. An excellent way to start, although it seems goofy, is to let your children "carpet" ski at home.

While you are skiing as a family, remember that your children cannot glide, turn, and fly downhill as you do, or would like to. Teach them carefully and slowly, never lecturing, always playing. Let children experiment and "discover" problems that you can help them with.

Trying to teach kick-and-glide techniques to children under 8 is ridiculous and frustrating. They would much rather be bounding around making snowmen, building igloos, and keeping warm. Let's face it, constantly falling down while getting tangled up in poles and skis is not exactly a rip-roarin' good time. Learn to set realistic goals for your children, especially the younger ones.

Those between the ages of 4 and 6 are still coping with balance and coordination, and have little long-term endurance. Any formalized lesson for children of this age should consist of plenty of fun and games with skis on and no poles. Tag, dodge ball, soccer (using hands to move the ball) and follow-the-leader are all very effective teaching aids. Children who are having a great time on skis naturally learn to balance and turn. Later on, these basic skills are easily adapted to a longer family outing.

Children of all ages, and even adults, fall down a lot. It is a part of learning. Teaching a child how to roll onto his or her back to untangle skis in the air is an important skill. Follow this by showing them how to place their skis parallel on the downhill side, roll forward onto their knees, and push up

Let your kids, expecially the younger ones, learn at their own pace.

from there. This one skill will save your children hours of exhausting effort and frustration.

Follow-the-leader is perhaps one of the easiest and most useful techniques to help your children master their skis. Leave your poles behind and begin to shuffle around. Lead them on a merry chase, but ever so slowly. Crouch down, stand up, side step, waddle, make stars in the snow, play tag, have fun.

As you encounter skills the children want to learn, use mime to teach them important techniques. "Walking like a duck" is useful when teaching uphill or herringbone technique. "Pretending to drive a car" is useful when teaching proper body positioning for going downhill.

As the children's skills increase and the level of adventure rises, your family will want to head out from the meadow. It is essential that you as a parent never forget that this is supposed to be fun. Always bring along plenty of water and snacks. It is good planning to pack along extra socks, mittens, a waterproof ground cloth for sitting on, lots of sunscreen, and a special hot drink as a surprise.

It is an excellent idea to plan a ski outing with another family. Your kids will have friends to play with and you can watch the children in shifts with the other parents.

Snowshoeing

Snowshoes have changed. Forget the old image of "waddle-waddle-quack-quack" and stumbling around on a pair of creations that resemble elongated garbage can lids.

Winter wanderers now find that snowshoes open up a world of possibility. Even a beginning snowshoer, or a family with children in tow, can travel over much more territory with much less effort than even experienced cross-country skiers. Why? Because snowshoes are stable and offer superior flotation and grip.

I can still remember my father a number of years ago returning cross-country skis politely to my shop and pointing curiously to a pair of snowshoes on the wall. I gave them to him and didn't see him again until just before sunset when he reappeared with a huge grin on his face.

Use a day pack as a stuffsack for your sleeping bag—that way you will have a pack to use on side trips.

In the wilderness, the best lunch is rarely a meal, but more a series of snacks that begins just after breakfast ends, and ends just as dinner begins.

Snowshoes are simple to use. With what is known in the industry as a "modified-H" style binding, your shoe or boot is held securely to the snowshoe using a combination toe holster and heel strap—relatively easy to put on and take off, even with gloved fingers.

Is your family looking for more exercise than just a walk in the woods? It's not a problem, since many of today's smaller profiles and narrower designs are intended for running. The technological advances in metal snowshoes allow the user to walk or even run normally. Even snowboarders are turning to snowshoes as a means of heading up into untracked snow for that all-important "virgin" run. Whether for running, cross-training, mountaineering, walking, or utilitarian footwear for working in deep snow on fence or trap-lines, every purchase must start in the same place—the store.

First off, consider the price. Adult sizes cost about $150 to $250 for a snowshoe-and-binding package. For a few dollars more you can add accouterments such as insulated bindings (for those really cold days) and heel cleats (for days when even a sure-footed snowshoe wants to act like a runaway train). Child-sized snowshoes, and shoes designed especially for children, typically made of molded high-density plastic, cost in the range of $40 to $50. They aren't as streamlined as the adult versions, but frankly, the children won't notice—they'll be too busy romping and stomping to care.

The old school of thought is that the longer and broader the snowshoe, the more buoyancy it provides, and therefore the more weight it can support. With that in mind, choosing the right size of wooden and laced snowshoes is done by re-

> The more you lash to the outside of your pack, the more unwieldy and unsteady the load will become.

A tent without mosquito netting is fine
as long as there are no mosquitoes.

lating existing snow conditions to your size and weight—and also to any weight you may be carrying. More weight and softer snow mean longer and wider snowshoes.

The advent of high-performance snowshoes has changed the picture somewhat, though. Snow conditions are the most important consideration now, depending on whether you're hiking alone or in a group. If you are hiking solo, you will be breaking trail, and you will need a shoe in the range of 9 × 30 or 10 × 36. If you are hiking in a group, and sharing trail breaking, flotation is less important so a shoe in the size range of 8 × 25 is appropriate. If you plan to run, and to use snowshoeing as a form of cross-training for aerobic benefits, you will want to purchase the smallest and lightest shoe possible.

If you are at all in doubt about how you will use the snowshoe, or what size is really best for you, don't buy straight away—rent your shoes. An increasing number of retail stores offer rentals, as do many ski resorts.

Once you have your snowshoes, no other gear is required. Standard hiking boots, or even running shoes (if you want a workout) are all the footwear you need. Dress in layers as you would for skiing, but be prepared to peel down to a minimum, as snowshoeing can work up quite a glow. If balance is a problem, or you just want additional security, opt for ski poles. One in each hand will offer four-point stability in awkward conditions.

There are a few basic technique considerations that may make your initial foray a little easier. Always switch off the lead when breaking trail, as it can be tiring and awkward. When you climb uphill, keep your weight over the balls of your feet.

Traversing a slope is more difficult, but can be accomplished by either "sawing" or "kicking" the uphill edge of your snowshoe into the snow.

Heading downhill means keeping your weight over the balls of the feet and being conscious of digging the binding cleats into the snow. Lean back, and you will "butt-slide" all the way down, for sure. As for level terrain, there isn't much more to it than putting one foot in front of the other.

Incidentally, let me gently remind you that ski trails are for skiers only. People on foot and snowshoers should keep off to the side of any established ski trail so as not to ruin the skiing.

Tips in a Nutshell

1. Buy skis that are too short rather than too long. Do not buy boots that are too large—instead take advantage of boot trade-in programs in stores.
2. Get professional ski lessons. When skiing with younger children who are just learning, play lots of games. Tag, fox and hares, follow-the-leader are great fun. Remember to ski slowly and allow the children to win frequently.
3. Keep ski or snowshoeing tours within everyone's endurance. Better to make outings too short than too long.
4. Pack plenty of wholesome snacks, water, and maybe a hot drink in a thermos flask. Hot chocolate or warmed cider are big favorites.
5. Pack extra socks, mittens, and hats.
6. Plan on skiing or snowshoeing with another family. You'll have additional adult supervision and the children will have playmates.
7. Remember to take plenty of breaks. Pack along strips of Ensolite and/or a ground cloth so everyone can stay warm and dry while sitting in the snow.

CHAPTER 7

Canoeing, Kayaking, and Rafting

Exploring the wilderness by canoe or kayak is a wonderful experience for a family. While you will be limited to relatively calm weather for most exploration, water trips present an opportunity for safe, enjoyable adventures in extremely beautiful surroundings. Paddling is a very comfortable way to transport yourself and your family. It is ideal for the family with young children who either cannot walk long distances or do not want to.

Traveling by boat does have its hazards, though. Heavy winds can whip up waves capable of overturning a canoe or kayak. A gentle river could surprise the paddler with unannounced rapids around a bend. Whatever the cause, it is enough to realize that you should not take your children on the water unless you yourself have acquired basic paddling skills and safety knowledge. Classes, clubs, and various demonstration days sponsored by manufacturers are excellent sources of information and instruction.

I also recommend that your children be able to float and tread water comfortably before you head out on a lake or river with them. There are many lessons offered by organizations such as the YMCA that help to "drown-proof" babies and children. Inquire at a local community pool for information.

Make sure your child is properly equipped and knows what to expect before heading downwriver.

Buying a canoe or kayak, paddles, life preservers, and other necessary gear can be expensive and confusing. Choosing what type of boat you want for your family is a personal and highly individual decision. No canoe or kayak is ideal under all circumstances. You have to make choices.

Will you be using the boat on flat water or white water? Will you be paddling rivers or lakes? How much weight and gear will the canoe or kayak be holding? How durable does it need to be? How much can you afford to spend? All these questions need to be answered before you make your choice. Although a canoe or kayak is expensive, it will last a lifetime with proper care.

If buying is too much for your family budget this year, try renting one. Many marinas and stores rent boats relatively cheaply. Most will require you either to demonstrate some level of competence in the craft or to take a lesson from them before letting you out on the open water.

Pack your food separately from your stove fuel—unless you particularly enjoy the flavor of white gas.

LIFE PRESERVERS

There are many safety factors to consider before you embark on a paddling trip, but none as important as wearing life preservers. Every person in the boat, even the smallest of children, must wear a Coast Guard–approved life preserver. These preservers should be designed so that they will keep a person floating upright and tilted slightly back, with the face supported out of water even when unconscious.

If you have any doubts about the effectiveness of a life preserver, have your child and other members of the family hang limp and totally relaxed in a pool while wearing the preserver. If they are not adequately supported by the preserver in the manner mentioned above, it is not safe. Also, be sure to check the fit and buoyancy every year as your children grow. What may have fit and supported their weight the year before may do nothing more than float them just below the surface this year.

CLOTHING

When you are dressing for a paddling trip, consider that when wet, the body will chill quite easily, even in a very slight breeze. While a bathing suit or a T-shirt and shorts are appropriate in warm sunny weather, always be sure to pack long pants, a warm sweater, wool socks, and a rain suit just in case. In cooler weather, layer accordingly, just as you would for cross-country skiing or hiking. Beware of cottons and wools that become extremely heavy when wet and tend to weigh a person down in the water.

Hats, sunglasses, and strong sunblock are absolute necessities when on the water. The sun's rays can be very intense

Store all your camping gear in a cool, dry place to avoid mildew and heat damage.

Unless you are trying to launch the space shuttle, running your stove on full-power all the time is a waste of fuel.

when reflected off the water and will burn a child's sensitive skin very easily. Don't forget to reapply sunscreen after swimming, and apply sunscreen under the ears and earlobes, under the chin, and under the nose. In a reflected sun, those areas are often overlooked and do burn easily.

Footwear is a tricky item. Tennis shoes work very well in warm water and warm weather, but feet will chill easily if the water is cold or the weather turns cool. If the shoes are big enough, putting on a pair of wool socks will help. Always pack an extra pair of shoes for everyone to wear when on shore. Hiking around in wet shoes is uncomfortable and potentially dangerous—wet shoes on slippery rocks are often a bruising combination. Old tennis shoes with holes in them for drainage are good for playing in water. Because of the possibility of hidden sharp rocks or sticks, I recommend that children always wear shoes when playing in the water.

Some companies make neoprene booties, rather like those divers wear, in small sizes with soles. These are super for walking as they keep the feet warm when wet, are light, and are easily slipped on. The drawback is that they keep the feet con-

Packing a firearm because you fear what is out there is not only unwise, it is illegal in many instances—besides, you probably wouldn't hit what you were shooting at anyway.

tinuously wet. There are other types of boating footwear or paddling shoes similar to slippers on the market that seem to work very well. Sandals are also good and can be worn with a warm pair of wool socks for insulation.

KEEPING GEAR DRY

Keeping your gear dry when boating is a serious concern. It is no fun to paddle for several hours, arrive at the campsite just before dusk, and find that your sleeping bags are soaked through because they were sitting in the bottom of the canoe. Retailers sell a variety of waterproof bags made of heavy nylon with a leak-proof seal that won't let water in even if all your gear gets dumped in the river.

For smaller items such as cameras and books, army-surplus ammunition cans work outstandingly well. I have several that have been painted orange for visibility (they are easier to spot floating in a river than are the green ones) and lined with old Ensolite for padding my camera gear. The ammunition cans have been through many rapids on whitewater rafting trips and have never let in a drop of water.

Other Considerations

Because children seem to enjoy boating, and because you can pack a large camp stove, kitchen equipment, a cooler, and lots of fresh food into a canoe, it does seem to be a perfect way to go camping with children. It is not without its drawbacks, however.

Children are naturally active. The younger the child, the shorter the attention span. Small kids can't sit still for long. Don't expect them to sit quietly in the boat for several hours while you paddle around. A certain amount of activity and entertainment is necessary to keep them happy while you're on

While a nip of rum in hot tea, or Kaluha in coffee, is outstanding, limit the intake of libations when outdoors as they cloud the judgment and can have adverse physical effects.

the water. You do not want them squirming around and making the boat unstable.

Luckily, it is not too difficult to keep children entertained and interested on the water. Just as with backpacking or hiking, activities need to be creative and varied—nothing works every time or all the time. Smaller children might like a tiny paddle that they can dip in and out of the water. They will not be much help, but it will not hamper your paddling efforts much, and it will make them feel like an important and active part of the excursion.

Many youngsters like to fish. Although this will usually work only if their parents like to fish as well, giving a child a fishing pole to use as you float along is great fun for them. Who knows, they may even catch the evening's dinner. But catching something isn't the point. As any wise fisherman will tell you, "It's the fishin' that's important, not the catchin'."

Staying close to shore is a super way to keep a child interested. This way, there will be lots of sand bars, undercut banks, and marshy areas for them to look at as you glide by. There is also an increased possibility of spotting wildlife. Imagine your child's amazement as you quietly slip by a large moose chewing river grasses, water dripping from its muzzle and weeds hanging from its antlers.

Hiking outdoors without wearing sunscreen is a bit like reaching into the oven without a mitt—you're going to get burned.

Be cautious when you choose your rafting outfitter—and ask plenty of questions.

Plan on plenty of shore breaks—one every 30 minutes is perfect. Children will not benefit from all-day paddling grinds to reach the ideal campsite. Just as you spent time playing on shore between leaving the car and loading the boat, your children will need playing time during a day-long paddle.

RAFTING TIPS

With hundreds of river-rafting companies, or outfitters, to choose from, finding the right whitewater outfitter means nothing more than asking the right questions.

Once you have perused your collection of catalogs and advertisement offerings and honed your list of outfitters down to a manageable few, give them a call and be prepared to ask a lot of questions.

Diane Strachan, former whitewater guide and public information officer for California Outdoors, the trade association of professional river outfitters, says that those outfitters willing to patiently spend time answering questions in a detailed and organized manner provide a good indicator of how smoothly the actual trip will run.

Nintendo, Sega, and Atari have no place in the outdoors.
If you need them, you may as well stay home.

Address points of safety first. How long has the river company been in business and how experienced are the guides? You don't want to experience your dream week on the river with a gang of novice guides working for a company that just blossomed out of some maverick's garage.

Find out if the outfitter is experienced in dealing with children and if they provide child-sized life jackets.

Strachan, a mother herself, recommends that families go rafting only with those companies that have demonstrated skill with children, which in itself is a safety factor since children are unpredictable.

Don't overlook questions regarding the client-to-guide ratio (6 guides to 24 guests is an absolute minimum) and the quality of the guides' wilderness-rescue and first-aid experience.

Inquire about the range of paddling difficulty offered and which trips the outfitter would recommend for someone with children.

Since there is much more to an enjoyable rafting adventure than rafts and water, take the time to investigate all the options available to you on a particular voyage. Natural-history walks, historical walks, wildflower hikes, and more are often bonuses on many whitewater trips.

Find out, too, what the paddling options are: paddle (you paddle), oar (the guide rows while you sit), or a combination. Check to see if the outfitter packs along inflatable kayaks for added fun and adventure.

If you have special dietary needs, now is the time to air those concerns to be sure the outfitter can adequately meet your requirements. When you are on the river, it is too late to find out that a no-salt menu isn't available.

Families will want to pay special attention to child-oriented activities. Does the guide provide bug cages, identification books, storytellers, special activities for children? Additionally, some outfitters, but not all, offer time-alone opportunities for parents while their children are being entertained.

One final note: If you're planning to embark on an extended rafting adventure, request a list of references. If the outfitter is unwilling or unable to provide them, take your business elsewhere.

Tips in a Nutshell

1. Never venture out on a lake or river without first acquiring basic paddling skills.
2. Everyone in the boat must wear a Coast Guard–approved life preserver. Be sure that each preserver floats the wearer feet-down, and face out of the water.
3. Dress warmly and in layers. Take extra clothing that everyone can change into in the event of getting soaked through. Clothing should be able to keep a person warm even when wet.
4. Apply generous amounts of sunscreen—don't forget the ear lobes, tip of the nose, and under the chin.
5. Wear shoes at all times—even in the water. Old tennis shoes with holes work well, as do specially made paddling shoes and sandals.
6. Keep valuables dry in army-surplus ammunition cans.
7. Keep driving distances to and from the boating site to a minimum—no more than 2 to 3 hours.
8. Keep children entertained by boating near the shore, giving them a small paddle or a fishing pole, and so on.
9. Take plenty of shore breaks.

CHAPTER 8

Touring by Bike

BICYCLE TOURING IS FEASIBLE WITH CHILDREN OF ANY AGE. Mountain biking, on the other hand, is best suited to older children. Mountain biking requires a strong sense of balance, agility, concentration, and a certain amount of stamina—traits not always found in children under the age of 10. Bicycling in general is a very adaptable sport, however. Paved bike paths, smooth dirt roads, and bike lanes on certain roads all provide an experience suitable for the family.

Near my home, in the San Francisco Bay area, there are excellent campgrounds with bike trails branching out from them. These trails, some paved, some dirt, allow my family and me to enjoy biking from the comfort of an established base camp.

Whatever type of cycling you have in mind for the family, there are some general considerations that apply. When choosing a bike for your child, check the length of the crank—the arm from the chain sprocket to the pedal. Most bike shops fit adults and children alike by having them straddle the frame with both feet flat on the ground. It is true that there should be at least an inch of clearance between the crotch and the top tube (two to three inches in mountain bikes). Smaller children may find the crank too long, however, even if the frame fits, and they will end up struggling to keep their feet

Don't skip snacks and water just because the weather is bad. Chilly, damp weather places more energy demands on your body, which needs extra food and water to create fuel.

on the pedals on the downstroke and hitting their chins with their knees on the upstroke. Make sure the bike you purchase has the right length of crank for your child.

The best multipurpose bike for younger children at this time is a BMX (bicycle motocross). Numerous manufacturers make them. Be sure you get one that is sturdy. Up to the age of 10, your child is best served by a single-speed bike. As your youngster's hands become larger and strong enough to work handbrakes, a more sophisticated 10-speed or mountain bike will be appropriate. Fat tires are more stable and versatile for children because they are not as concerned with aerodynamics or speed for the moment. Stay away from banana-style seats as they tend to distribute the child's weight unevenly over the bike and interfere with balance.

Helmets for everyone in the family are mandatory. Children's heads usually stop growing after the age of 5, so a helmet purchased at this time can reasonably be expected to last 4 to 5 years, or until the child is about 10. Up until the time a

A clean sleeping bag is a warm one. Follow the manufacturer's directions for cleaning.

The best cure for altitude sickness, dehydration, heat exhaustion, hypothermia, and so on, is prevention. Learn what steps to take.

child's head stops growing, buy a helmet with growth adjustment built in. Some children are a bit stubborn about wearing a helmet but in most cases they will follow a parent's lead, so put your helmet on first and the child is likely to follow. If not, then get off the bike and the trip is over. Under no circumstances should you allow your child to ride without a helmet.

Children under the age of 7 will most likely be unable to pedal their own bike alongside parents for any length of time, certainly for not much more than a tour of the neighborhood, so they will have to ride with you. You must decide between a bicycle seat and a trailer. If you choose a seat that fixes to your machine, make sure it is made of sturdy plastic with a high backrest, armrests, spoke protectors, seat belts, and a chest harness. Child seats will do nicely up to the age of 4 years, but after that either children must pedal on their own bike or you must consider adding a trailer. When you are carrying a child in the seat, be sure to watch your speed and control. This is important not only for your child's safety, but for your safety and comfort as well.

Trailers, although somewhat expensive, are a very safe and stable alternative to bike seats. There are several different styles on the market so choose carefully. Should the children face forward or back? Should the trailer be of plastic or aluminum? Do you want a roof for weather protection? Do you want the trailer to attach to the frame, or near the seat? The frame attachment allows the bike to fall without tipping the cart.

Once you have assembled and attached the bike trailer, be sure to make it extremely visible to drivers by displaying an

Keep your traveling groups small and be considerate toward other trail users.

Trailers are a safe, though expensive, alternative to child seats. And a trailer can haul extra gear as well.

orange safety flag on a 6-foot wand attached to the right rear corner of the trailer.

If you have only one child, there will be room in the trailer for camping gear, reducing the pannier load and rear-wheel drag considerably. Trailers can haul up to 100 pounds of gear without too much difficulty or strain on the pedaler.

Before starting your first trip with a trailer or child seat, get thoroughly used to pedaling with extra weight. This is especially advisable if you are planning a family bike-camping trip and the bikes are loaded down with panniers as well. Extra weight will affect the way a bike rides, and its stability. Braking takes longer, hills seem steeper, and corners must be taken more carefully.

As your children get older they will become skilled and strong enough to be able to venture out with you on longer tours. It is crucial that they thoroughly understand the rules of the road and can positively control their bikes, even if you

Biodegradable toilet paper is great, as long as you still either pack it out or burn it in the campfire.

are just riding off-road. Make sure they know and practice these rules:

- Ride with traffic.
- Stop before entering a street.
- Stop at all stop signs and red lights.
- Look over your shoulder and wait for overtaking traffic before turning left.
- Avoid oncoming traffic as well.
- Don't play around in the road.

More rules for mountain bikes are given on page 113.

Bikers often express a fear of dogs. I have had very few bad experiences with dogs, but it is wise to be prepared. Sprays, loud horns, clubs, and so on, are not necessarily good weapons to use when you're being chased by a dog. Quite often these methods only anger the dog. The best course of action is to dismount from the bike and walk. This will give the dog a chance to see you as a human. With careful scooting and leaping you should be able to keep the bike between you and even the most unfriendly of beasts. If dismounting doesn't do the trick, you might have to use a spray repellent in the dog's face after all, or give it a sharp whack over the snout with your tire pump.

Assuming you like to see where you are going and value your vision, we recommend that you wear sunglasses when outdoors in the sun.

Always take plenty of water, a tire pump, a first-aid kit, a small tool kit, a spare tube, a tire-patch kit, snacks, and extra clothing. I also recommend wearing bike gloves to pad and protect your hands.

There is a wide variety of specialized clothing on the market for bikers, but much of it is not absolutely necessary. Bike shorts and bike shoes are well worth the investment, however. The well-dressed rider wears cycling gloves, riding shorts, stiff-soled riding shoes, sunglasses, helmet, and a T-shirt. For weather changes or emergencies you should also carry a windbreaker and thermal underwear.

MOUNTAIN BIKE RULES

- Ride on open trails only. Please respect and abide by all trail closures, private property notices and fences, and all requirements for use permits and authorization. Mountain bikes are never permitted within wilderness areas, or on any section of the Pacific Crest Trail, most national park trails, and many state park trails. Don't assume a trail is legal for mountain bikes just because it is not signed—inquire before pedaling.
- Leave no trace. Do not skid your tires or ride on ground that is rain-soaked and easily scarred. Stick to established trails.
- Control your bicycle. Save the "need for speed" for a race. Stay alert at all times. Speed and an out-of-control mountain biker lead to trouble and often injury to other trail users. Anticipate that others may be just around a blind corner.
- Always yield right of way. Mountain bikes are low-man on the totem pole and must always yield trail to horses and hikers. When encountering other trail users (hikers, equestrians, or fellow bikers) a friendly greeting to announce your presence is considerate and appreciated. One unfriendly or negative encounter with a mountain biker leaves a lasting impression on all other trail users. Slow to a walk or stop your bike, especially when encountering horses.

- Never spook animals. Leave ranch and farm gates as you find them. Running livestock and disturbing wild animals can cause serious harm and in most instances is considered a major offense. Give them plenty of room.
- Plan ahead. Know your equipment, know your ability, know the requirements of the area you are riding in, and then plan accordingly. Be self-sufficient at all times.
- Narrow or single-track trails are used by everyone—keep your speed under control so that you may be able to stop well before causing a hiker to dive off the trail.

Tips in a Nutshell

1. Be sure the crank length on your child's bike is appropriate.
2. Everyone must wear a helmet at all times—no helmet, no ride, period. A good pair of bike shorts and riding gloves are also recommended.
3. Before heading out with a child seat on your bike, or a trailer in tow, practice getting used to the added weight and drag. Your turning ability and stopping ability will be different.
4. If your child is in a seat or carrier, some sort of head support will give him or her a more comfortable ride when he or she inevitably falls asleep and the head goes limp.
5. Be very sure that your children understand and practice safe rules for the road or trail before they are allowed to pedal along on any outing.
6. Pack along a compact bike repair kit as well as water, snacks, first-aid kit, tire pump, and tire-patch kit.
7. Be sure to bring a windbreaker and some warm clothes to put on in the event the weather changes.

CHAPTER 9

First Aid and Safety

THE BEST FIRST AID IS PREVENTION. JUST AS YOU WOULD SPEND time teaching your children to say no to drugs and to be cautious of strangers, you should spend time teaching them outdoor safety. Although teaching children safety in the outdoors is potentially tricky (you don't want to scare them out of the wilderness), it is important to be honest and frank.

Teaching children to be cautious around fire, sharp objects, and camp hazards, such as tent guy lines, is fairly basic, but important. There are, however, more subtle hazards that children should know how to identify.

Specific Dangers

ROCKS, RUBBLE, BRUSH PILES, AND FALLEN LOGS

Loose rocks could give way, causing a slip and a sprained ankle. Rocks also can slide, creating a much more dangerous situation. Rubble, brush piles, and logs can all give way when weight is placed upon them, and lead to open wounds, broken bones, and bruises. It is also possible for supports to give way and shift, trapping the unfortunate victim. Children love to climb on fallen logs—so do adults—but caution is important. Loose bark, moss, and debris all can lead to a nasty fall.

I know everyone has heard the phrase, "Put that down or you will put someone's eye out!" Protecting the face when traveling through dense underbrush, walking at a safe distance behind the person ahead, and watching out that branches are not snapped back in the face of someone following behind will do much to prevent eye injury.

TREES

Climbing in trees is great fun, but care must be exercised. Teach children to look for weak or dead branches that might break under their weight. Moss growing on branches could cause a slip. Never break branches or pull branches out of trees for firewood, unless it's an emergency. It is not friendly to the environment and invites potential injury by pulling the tree down or starting an avalanche of broken branches.

WATER, MUD, WET SAND, AND RIVER BANKS

Water attracts children like a picnic attracts ants. Children should be instructed not to go near water without adult supervision, and even then only where it is slow-moving and very shallow. Potential hazards exist that must be identified. Mud and wet sand on a river bank or the edge of a lake is sometimes quite deep. A headlong sprint to the water without first checking the mud or sand could result in a child's becoming stuck, making rescue very difficult.

River banks often give way without notice. Teach your children the dangers of sitting or standing on the edge of high river banks that may be undercut by the water flow. Also teach them that any time the water is moving swiftly, the river

Carry a first-aid kit consisting only of gear you know how to use.

Take the time to learn basic first-aid skills.

Carrying a map and compass is important—
knowing how to use them is essential.

N W E S

banks are suspect. If a river bank gives way and pitches a child into rapids or cold, deep, water, he or she could drown or suffer severe hypothermia.

SNOW AND ICE

Snow and ice present another range of hazards. It is important to teach your children to stay alert in snowy or icy conditions. Snow-covered trees, rocky ledges, and ice overhangs all can give way without notice, burying everything underneath them. Snow at the top of ravines or on ridges is unstable. Snow also melts into clothing causing chilling, which may lead to hypothermia. Ice is deceptive, too. Stay away from ice-covered lakes, rivers, river banks, and ponds. There really is no safe way to determine the strength of the ice, and a fall into icy water can be deadly.

POISONOUS PLANTS

Older children are likely to come into contact with poison oak, poison ivy, or poison sumac (see page 133 later in this chapter). Not all of these plants grow in every area of the United States, so you should check with your local park service. Children should know how to identify leaflet clusters and color so they can avoid the nasty skin reaction that results from contact with these plants.

Younger children, must also be taught not to test berries, mushrooms roots, leaves, and plants by tasting them. They are all inviting to the young eye and palate but many are poisonous.

You can't out-climb, out-swim, or out-run a bear. Your best defense is alertness. Never mess with a mother bear's cubs—she will aggressively defend her young.

NETTLES

Nettles in the woods can deliver a sting to your bare skin. On some people, a nasty welt and severe itching or burning kick in almost immediately. The treatment is fairly simple. Wash the afflicted area thoroughly with soap and water. Applying a mild antiseptic or lotion also can relieve itching. Aloe vera ointments or gel will relieve the burning sensation. The best bet, of course, is to anticipate that your children will be walking through areas that may be overgrown with nettles, and to make them wear protective clothing.

ANIMALS AND INSECTS

Inform your children about poisonous animals, insects, and other hazards, but don't scare them. The idea is to instill caution and respect, not fear. When you talk to your children about animals, educate them with the fullest picture that you can provide; sometimes this may require a bit of research on your part, either alone or with your child. To say that bears are dangerous and then leave it at that is insufficient. Children should learn all you are able to share. You may even have to remove the Hollywood image from their conception of animals. Read books together, go to museums and zoos, anything to present the most complete picture possible.

The more your child learns, and the more you learn, too, for that matter, the better. If you and your children are knowledgeable and alert, you will rarely be bothered by a "dangerous" animal.

First Aid

The information in this chapter on first-aid materials and procedures is not a substitute for trained medical assistance in an emergency or otherwise. Whenever possible, seek medical help. The value of a first-aid kit is much reduced in the hands of an untrained person; in fact more harm can be caused than good done. Using drugs improperly or inappropriately, or failing to recognize immediate requirements, causes needless injuries and even deaths every year. *Everyone in your family should become trained in first aid and cardiopulmonary resuscitation (CPR).* Excellent programs are offered by the Red Cross, the American Heart Association, and private organizations or hospitals. Organizations such as the Sierra Club or other outdoor clubs offer wilderness first-aid courses. Become trained. Become safe.

The following information is neither intended to be training in first aid, nor an endorsement of techniques or products. Consult your doctor or local library, and become trained and certified in first-aid before assembling a first-aid kit for the outdoors.

All that notwithstanding, let me put your mind at ease. First aid is the practice of common sense, nothing more, nothing less. In my years of teaching wilderness first aid, I have witnessed some of the finest first aid performed by relatively untrained individuals. They didn't reach into a drug bag and begin administering medicine, nor did they do anything tricky or fancy. What they did was remain calm and at ease.

During insect season, seek higher ground away from streams and bodies of water. Higher ground means stronger breezes that will help to keep the squadrons of little peskies at bay.

Hike in light-colored clothing. Studies have shown that mosquitoes are more readily attracted to dark colors.

They provided comfort and tended to the needs of the injured parties as best they could. That is the essence of first aid—do good if you can, but do no harm.

Before heading out into the wilderness with your children, it is important that they learn some simple first-aid skills as well. Should something happen to an adult, the children will need some first-aid skills, no matter how basic, and the confidence to perform them. Children should never have to feel helpless. Practice in the house, backyard, or nearby park. The more the child knows, the more independently and confidently he or she will begin looking at emergency or stressful situations. More importantly, they will learn how to prevent injury in the first place.

There are some basics that govern action for most first-aid procedures. First is finding out how the injury occurred, and then making sure no one else in the group, including the potential rescuer, will also be injured. Second is to remove the mechanism of injury from the injured party if it is life-threatening. This may involve moving the victim, but only if the immediate situation really is life-threatening, and under no other circumstances. Any time you move anyone, you risk causing more damage, which could result in permanent injury or death.

Third, perform the ABCs.

A: Be sure the *Airway* is not blocked or compromised in any way.

B: Evaluate *Breathing*. Watch the rise and fall of the chest.

C: Check for *Circulation*. See if the person has a pulse.

If the answer is no to any of the ABCs, you must begin rescue breathing or CPR. It is important to realize that you can perform this third step almost simultaneously with step two. Establishing an airway and performing CPR can be performed effectively while transporting the patient out of immediate danger—don't get caught wasting precious seconds.

Fourth, control bleeding by first applying direct pressure to the wound, using the hand to hold a dressing in place. A clean article of clothing, a bandanna, sanitary napkin, whatever clean cloth or absorbent material is available, will work as a dressing. Add dressings to the wound while maintaining pressure until the bleeding stops. If the stack of dressings becomes too bulky or ineffective, remove from the top, but do not remove the one that is in direct contact with the wound as you risk starting the bleeding all over again.

Fifth, stabilize any other injuries such as fractures and dislocations to prevent further discomfort and harm. Never try to set a fracture or restore a dislocation. This is sometimes done in the wilderness, but only to save life and only by trained personnel. Creating a calm and comfortable environment for the injured person while attending to injuries is essential.

Sixth, always treat the victim for shock. Shock is life-threatening, even if the injury is not. Shock can result from allergic reaction, from a severe or not-so-severe injury, from poisoning, or as a result of illness or seeing someone else injured. Some of the classic signs and symptoms of shock are weakness, pale color, cool and clammy skin, irregular breathing patterns, nausea, dizziness, and shivering, even in warm weather. It is important to maintain the injured party's temperature. Wrap the person in an emergency blanket, sleeping bag, or extra clothing if the weather is cold. In hot weather, keep the person cool by creating shade. Always attempt to keep the individual insulated from the ground. As a rule, keep the injured party lying down, comfortable, and resting with the feet raised. In the event of a head injury, do not raise the feet. Listen to the injured party and meet their needs, do not try to restrain them in an attempt to "do what the book says." If they feel more comfortable sitting up, then let them. However, do continue to encourage them to rest and keep warm.

WATER PURIFICATION

Your backcountry water might look pure, but that doesn't mean it is. If you leave your water filter behind to save weight, harmful organisms such as giardia and cryptosporidium can cause nausea, diarrhea, vomiting, or worse. Consequently, a water filter is essential for outdoor travel. And these days, there's no excuse for going without one. Handheld filters are becoming more compact, lighter, and easier to use. You'll find filters ranging in price from $25 to $300. Unless your needs are very basic and very temporary, you'll find that filters costing $50 and more offer the best deal in terms of versatility, durability, and function.

The goal of a filter is to strain out microscopic contaminants. A filter with a rating of one micron or smaller will remove protozoa such as giardia and cryptosporidium, as well as parasitic eggs and larva, but it takes a pore size of less than 0.4 micron to remove bacteria.

If you travel in third-world countries you'll have viruses to deal with as well. And no matter where you are, if you encounter water contaminated by sewage, it, too, will contain viruses. Only one filter I know of, the First Need, by General

It is fine to take risks as long as you are also willing to accept the consequences of those risks and not endanger other people as a result.

Ecology, claims to meet federal virus-removal standards by filtration alone, thanks to a fancy matrix system. The others require chemical assistance, either by incorporating iodine in the filter or by using iodine tablets such as Potable Aqua.

Iodine tastes awful and may affect some people adversely, so many filters using iodine also have a carbon element to remove the iodine when its job is done. Carbon gets rid of pesticides, herbicides, heavy metals, and chlorine, but there are some disadvantages to using carbon. Some recent studies have shown that in certain situations it's best to leave a little iodine intact. If you believe your water source is contaminated with sewage, you'll want to remove the carbon filter. I've found that orange juice crystals (ascorbic acid) can help offset the iodine's nasty taste, but if you follow my lead, remember to wait a half-hour after filtering before stirring it in. In addition, that carbon element has a limit for absorbing a particular chemical. Once that limit is reached, it lets the bad stuff through. Always replace the filter and the carbon element according to the manufacturer's recommended schedule.

A good backcountry water filter weighs less than 20 ounces, is easy to grasp, simple to use, and a snap to clean and maintain. At the very least, buy one that removes protozoa and bacteria. (A number of cheap, pocket-sized filters remove only giardia and cryptosporidium. That, in my book, is risking your health to save money.) Consider the flow rate, too: A liter per minute won't leave you dying for a drink.

All filters will eventually clog—it's a sign that they've been doing their job. If you force water through a filter that's becoming difficult to pump, you risk injecting a load of microbes into your bottle. Some models can be brushed, or scrubbed, as ceramic elements are, to extend their useful lives. And if the filter has a pre-filter to screen out the big stuff, use it. It will make your filter last longer—possibly 100 gallons per disposable element. Finally, each filter has its own idiosyncrasies and needs, so be sure to read the manufacturer's instructions carefully.

If you don't feel like carrying the weight or bulk of a filter, you can opt for chemical treatments such as iodine or you can boil the water. Boiling is virtually foolproof but it takes time and a considerable amount of fuel. Additionally, I have yet to meet an adult or child who enjoys drinking hot water on a hot day. Iodine has worked well for me and I have been very happy with either Polar Pure (an iodine crystal–based system) or Potable Aqua (a tablet). Since Potable Aqua is a tablet system, it is quite easy for children to understand and use if necessary, although it does have a very limited shelf life once the bottle is open. Polar Pure has a much longer shelf life and is more versatile, but it may be more complicated to use.

ALTITUDE SICKNESS

Altitude sickness is the body's reaction to reduced oxygen supplies. The higher the elevation, the thinner the air and the more likely the body is to succumb to altitude sickness, although it's more common at 8,000 feet or higher. The symptoms are nausea, headache, shortness of breath, and extreme fatigue. Rest, food, and water are the only cure because the body takes time to acclimate to altitude change. Descending a few thousand feet usually brings fast relief. The odds of getting altitude sickness are greatly reduced by drinking water, eating well, and gaining altitude gradually.

BLISTERS

Blisters are caused by friction or constant uncomfortable binding pressure—usually from a poorly fitting boot or inadequately protected feet. To lessen the chance of getting foot blisters, assuming your boots fit properly, I recommend the following:

1. Use two pairs of socks—one thin liner and a thicker, cushioning outer sock of wool.
2. Take the time to remove debris that has fallen in your boot.
3. Never hike for extended periods with wet feet.

If you experience discomfort or a hot spot, stop immediately and attend to your feet. If there is evident redness, but no blister, applying moleskin directly to the hot spot should take care of the discomfort. If a blister has begun to form, cut a doughnut out of molefoam and surround the blister. Secure the foam with a strip of moleskin if necessary.

If the blister is broken, treat it as an open wound. Clean the area with soap and water and then dress accordingly. I have found that applying SecondSkin, a gelatin-like sheet, directly over the broken blister and securing it in place with moleskin works well.

You may find that if the feet are dirty and somewhat sweaty, moleskin or adhesive tape will peel off or not stick well to the skin. You can overcome this by cleaning the area with an alcohol wipe, then applying tincture of benzoin around, but not on, the wound. This will prepare the skin for an application of adhesive.

BURNS

Minor burns such as those received from a hot stove, a pot handle, or a match are usually not serious enough to warrant medical attention. Nevertheless, you should treat them seriously. Immerse the affected part in cool water to alleviate the

Seek shelter away from a mountain peak or an exposed ridge during lightning or a thunderstorm.

pain and stop the burning sensation. Clean the area with soap and water and consider the application of a topical anesthetic to lessen pain.

For more severe burns involving blistering and deep-tissue damage, the victim will need medical attention.

BRUISES

Bruising is caused by a blow to the muscle or soft tissue, resulting in internal bleeding which, in turn, causes swelling and discoloration. If the swelling and pain increase dramatically over a 24-hour period, then a visit to the nearest emergency room is a wise precaution. Otherwise, resting the extremity in an elevated position with a cold, but not wet, compress application, is appropriate.

CUTS, LACERATIONS, AND INCISIONS

The best first aid for an open wound is to cleanse the area with anti-bacterial soap and water. Apply a clean, non-adhering dressing, such as a Telfa pad, and secure it with adhesive tape. For serious bleeding, apply direct pressure to the wound with a clean sterile compress. Elevate the wound above the level of the heart, if necessary, to slow the bleeding. Continue to apply direct pressure and add more compresses to the original dressing until the bleeding slows or stops. When bleeding has stopped, secure the wound with a compression bandage and head to the hospital for stitches.

Wounds should be sewn up within six hours to lessen scarring, so do not allow the wound to get too old or too dirty. Steristrips or butterfly bandages can be used as interim stitches to hold incisions or lacerations together until surgical stitches can be inserted. The wound must be clean and antiseptic before using Steristrips, if at all possible.

It is appropriate to apply an antibacterial ointment to the dressing before applying it to the wound. This will help prevent infection, a major concern with all wounds. Puncture wounds and abrasions are the most likely to become infected because there is little bleeding to flush away embedded dirt. Lacerations create a fair amount of torn and dead skin and are also very likely to become infected. Always clean a wound with soap and water.

EYE PROBLEMS

If any chemical contaminants such as stove fuel or chlorine get in the eye, flush it with large amounts of water. Be sure to flush from the inside corner of the eye (the one nearest the nose) outward, so you don't get the contaminant on your face or in your other eye. Keep irrigating for 10 to 15 minutes until you are sure the chemical has been removed. Use a continuous gentle stream of water and not a blast, such as that from a garden hose. After irrigating the eye, remove any coagulated chemical from the eye with a moistened cloth. Irrigate the eye again. Do not put medications in the eye. Cover the injured eye with a sterile gauze pad and immediately take the victim to the hospital.

In the case of a puncture wound, do not remove the object if it is still in the eye. Create a doughnut from a bandanna and place it around the injured eye to make a raised protective surface. You can then bandage the eye without the risk of pushing on the object. Incidentally, you will need to bandage both eyes, so the injured party is not tempted to move them and cause greater pain and damage. Evacuate to a hospital immediately.

IMPALED OBJECTS

In the event of getting a fishhook stuck in the flesh you will have to push the hook's barbed end all the way through the skin, clip it off, and then pull the shaft back through. This is very painful and it sometimes helps if you deaden the area with a local anesthetic, such as lidocaine, or ice. If at all possible, this procedure should be performed in an emergency room.

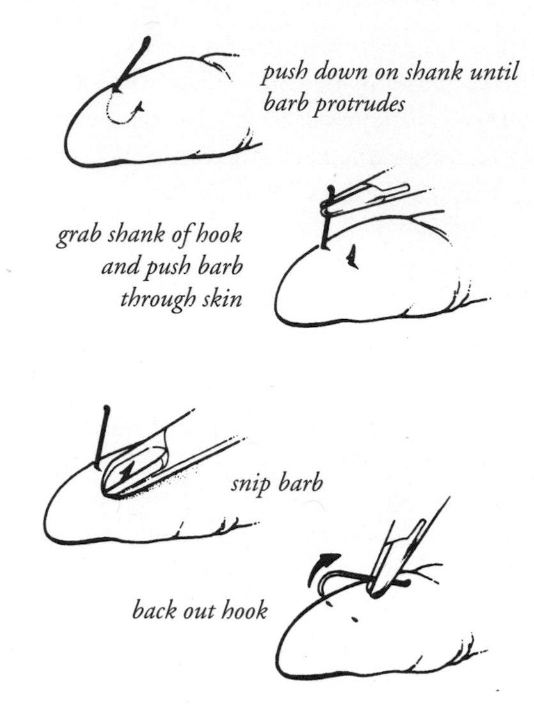

Removing a fishhook using the "push and snip technique."
(William Hamilton)

Sometimes the hook is in a position that allows for easier removal:

Cut the line from the hook. Loop a piece of fairly stout fishing line around the exposed bend of the hook, holding the two tag ends in one hand. Press the thumb of your other hand down firmly on the eye of the hook. In one very quick, strong motion, yank the loop of line in the direction opposite the line of the hook's entry. Removed in this fashion, there's rarely more than a drop of blood and no further injury.

Incidentally, it's a good idea, especially when you are fishing in the wilderness with kids, to flatten the barb against the shank with pliers.

> Peek at your pee. If your body is producing relatively clear urine five times a day, your fluid intake is fine. Cloudy or dark urine and an urge to pee fewer than five times a day mean you need more to drink.

HEAT-INDUCED EXHAUSTION, STROKE, AND CRAMPS

Heat exhaustion is caused by the loss of important bodily fluids and salt, usually in a hot environment. This can be prevented by eating correctly, drinking two to four quarts of fluid per day, reducing physical activity during very hot weather, and perhaps by adding an electrolyte to your drinking water, such as ERG, or BodyFuel. The symptoms are dizziness, pale skin, restlessness, nausea, rapid heartbeat, and headache. Treat by cooling the patient—taking off clothing, getting into shade, and so on. Sponge the victim with water. Give sips of fluid to drink, fortified with an electrolyte or salt. Be careful that in initiating the cooling process you don't send the victim into a hypothermic state.

Heat stroke is far more dangerous and the onset much more sudden. Confusion, irrational behavior, rapid pulse and respiration, hot and dry skin, and unconsciousness are common symptoms. To treat, clothing should be removed and the body moistened with cool water and fanned to increase air circulation and evaporative cooling. Again, beware not to overcool the body into a hypothermic state. Removal to a hospital is necessary.

Muscle cramps are most often caused by a shortage of salt in the body fluids, usually because of heavily worked muscles. Drinking too much water without salt may contribute to the problem. Fluids fortified with electrolytes will help prevent painful cramps. The site of a cramp should be massaged and stretched, but muscle soreness is likely for several days afterward.

HYPOTHERMIA AND FROSTBITE

Hypothermia occurs when the body loses more heat than it can generate. The difference between mild and severe hypothermia is very difficult to recognize unless you have a thermometer that reads below 94°F. Hypothermia is very difficult to treat, but it is much easier to prevent. Follow these rules:

- Eat a balanced diet.
- Drink adequate amounts of fluid.
- Dress for the weather.
- Keep your body and clothing dry by controlling sweating and preventing outside moisture from seeping in.
- Cover your head, neck, and hands.
- Wear clothes that will maintain insulative properties even when wet.

Wearing wet clothing, sitting on snow, and allowing a cold wind to blow on a body moist with perspiration are all invitations to hypothermia.

A mildly hypothermic person will complain of cold, may have difficulty performing simple motor functions, may become apathetic, may be shivering, and will have a body core temperature down to 95°F. Move the patient to a warm place, remove damp clothing or add warm insulation, and—if the victim is fully conscious and able to swallow easily—offer warm liquids and food.

For moderate to severe hypothermia, the victim will exhibit slurred speech, stumbling, unresponsiveness, decreased pulse and respiration, mental confusion, and unconsciousness. The body core temperature will be below 95°F. End the exposure immediately by covering the victim. Do not allow the victim to walk or move, and handle him or her very gently. Movement may force cold blood from the limbs into the core of the body, further complicating the situation. Incidentally, never administer alcoholic drinks to anyone suffering from hypothermia of any degree. They could be killers.

Check the victim for signs of frostbite—see instructions following. If no hospital is within quick reach, you will have to rewarm the patient, even though it is tricky and must be done slowly and with great care. Focus on applying warmth to the head, neck, armpits, and groin. Heat will most easily reach the body core from these areas. Use warm water bottles and warm blankets. If you have a double sleeping bag, climb in with the patient, and let your body heat do the work. Do not apply outside heat to the arms or legs. Take great care not to burn the victim. In all situations of potential hypothermia, it's essential to believe—and act on—the signs and symptoms, even if the victim doesn't believe them.

Frostbite is caused when blood circulation is restricted or stopped in extremities such as fingers and toes. This allows the water in the tissues to freeze. Your job is to prevent additional freezing and further damage to the tissue that could result from thawing and then refreezing. The symptoms are white skin that is waxy and hard to the touch; skin that feels intensely cold and numb; restricted movement in joints; and, in severe frostbite, hardness of underlying tissue.

Give the victim plenty of fluids. Don't warm the affected part if it is going to bear weight and will refreeze, and don't rub or massage the area. Evacuate to a hospital.

INSECT BITES AND STINGS

Unless the victim suffers an allergic reaction, bites and stings are usually more painful than they are serious. For bee stings, use a knife edge or fingernail to scrape out the stinger. Do not use tweezers or try to grab the stinger, because you may squeeze more venom into the sting area. Wash the affected area with soap and water and daub on anti-sting lotion, CamphoPhenique, or a paste of baking soda and water. If the area begins to itch badly, apply a lotion such as calamine.

Victims suffering allergic reactions should be given an antihistamine. Keep them calm, make sure the airway remains open, and take them to the hospital. People who know that they are allergic will often carry an Ana-Kit, which contains a premeasured injection to fight the reaction. **For more on dealing with insects, see Appendix VII beginning on page 176.**

DEALING WITH NOSEBLEEDS

To treat a nosebleed, keep the patient sitting and apply pressure on the side that is bleeding for at least five minutes. Another suggested method is to pinch the nose just below the bridge and hold it for five minutes with the head tilted back. If this does not stop the bleeding, pack the nostril with soft cotton, gauze, or tissue. Sometimes combining this with cold packs on the bridge of the nose will help. When the bleeding stops, the patient must continue resting and not blow the nose or pick at the encrusted blood. If you are not able to staunch the bleeding in this manner, a visit to the nearest emergency room becomes necessary.

INGESTED POISONS

When poisoning is suspected, it is important to seek medical assistance immediately. Find out, if possible, what has caused the poisoning and contact the poison control center for instructions. If help is not immediately available, there are some steps that can be taken. First be sure the person is breathing and that there is a pulse. If not, you will need to begin CPR. Use caution in giving mouth-to-mouth resuscitation because it is possible for the rescuer to become poisoned as well—especially if the victim vomits the substance into the rescuer's mouth, which does happen.

Here is a helpful rule of thumb:

Do not induce vomiting when the substance ingested contained petroleum, acid, or alkali.

Another way to put it is this: If it burned on the way down, it will burn on the way up—so do not induce vomiting.

Diluting any poison based on petroleum, acid, or alkali is thus not an option, because it will make the victim vomit.

For poisoning by medicine or plants, however, dilution is acceptable, as is inducing vomiting.

As usual, the best first aid for poisoning is prevention. Teach your children not to eat plants and berries or put things into their mouths. Also, be sure all substances are clearly labeled and easily identified. If a fuel bottle containing white gas looks similar to a water bottle, you are asking for trouble.

POISON OAK, IVY, AND SUMAC

These plants are regional, so find out which ones grow in your area and learn to identify them. Normally, poison ivy and sumac grow in the midwestern and eastern states, and poison oak only in the West. Poison oak and ivy both go by the rule: "Leaflets three, let them be." The main differences are that poison oak is a tree or shrub, and poison ivy is a vine. Also, poison oak leaves are lobed, while poison ivy leaves are somewhat jagged. Poison sumac is a shrub that grows mostly in swampy areas and has smooth leaves growing in a single line along each stem and opposite each other. All the plants secrete urushiol, a noxious oil that severely irritates the skin. It can be transmitted by direct contact, contact with contaminated clothing or pets, or breathing the smoke.

Signs appear within a day or two of contact. The skin will burn, itch, or both; become blistered; and sometimes swell. If the oils have been inhaled, breathing may become very difficult. This is an emergency and will require medical treatment.

If you suspect you have contacted any of these poisonous

A walk in the woods will at some point introduce your child to these three troublesome plants. Teach them how to identify each.
(William Hamilton)

plants, first remove all contaminated clothing and wash it separately. Second, wash the skin with soap (use a strong laundry soap or detergent) and water. Use warm, not hot, water. Wipe the affected area with rubbing alcohol.

If a rash develops, avoid scratching because opening the blisters can lead to secondary infection. Contrary to belief, the ooze from a broken blister does not contain urushiol and will not spread the rash. Apply cold compresses, a soothing lotion, or both, containing hydrocortisone or a similar agent.

Put together an emergency repair kit
for your equipment.

SNAKEBITES

The danger from snakebites is blown out of proportion. In the United States there are four kinds of poisonous snakes: rattlesnakes, copperheads, water moccasins, and coral snakes. These snakes will strike only if irritated, scared, or surprised and left without an escape route. They bite humans in defense, not offense. Human beings are not, and will never be, food for a snake.

Learn to identify the snakes in your area and where they like to live. In more than 20 years of exploring and hiking all over the United States, Canada, and Baja California, Mexico, I have seen fewer than 20 poisonous snakes. Remember, too, that many recorded snakebites occurred because the snake was being handled.

Snakebite kits are of little use. In most cases, you'll do more harm with a "slice and dice" kit than would have occurred had the victim just been taken to a hospital. If you insist on carrying a snakebite kit, I recommend one that provides powerful suction and does not involve cutting. Never apply a tourniquet or ice, and never use your mouth for suction.

Most experts agree that this is the recommended first aid for snakebite:

- Try to identify the snake, so the correct antivenin can be administered quickly. But do not waste time chasing the snake and do not try to catch or kill it.
- Clean the wound.

- Immobilize the injured limb below heart level and keep the victim calm.
- Apply a pressure bandage directly over the bite area.
- Get the victim to a hospital as soon as possible.

SPRAINS AND STRAINS

Sprains are caused by a sudden twisting or wrenching of a joint, the result of a hit or fall. The most commonly sprained joints are the wrist, knee, and ankle. It is almost impossible to distinguish between a break and a sprain without an X ray, so a first-aider should always assume the limb is broken. Elevate and immobilize the injured limb to relieve pain and prevent further injury. The application of a cold pack is appropriate and will help keep down swelling.

Strains most commonly occur in muscles that have been overused. The back, neck, arms, and legs all get a lot of work when you're carrying a backpack—often more than the body is ready for if you spend most of your time in an office. Children seem less susceptible to strains, although they get them too. An application of gentle heat, massage, and rest should help.

SUNBURN

Prevention is the best cure for sunburn. Sunblock or sunscreen should be applied to all areas of exposed skin. Remember that the higher the elevation, the more intense the sun. Always use a lotion with a sun protection factor (SPF) of 15 or more. For younger children, and those with very sensitive skin, I recommend 25 SPF or greater.

Wear a hat with a wide brim that protects the scalp, face, and neck. Always wear sunglasses, especially in higher altitudes and snowy conditions. Sunburned (snow-blind) eyes are not only painful, they are dangerous.

If the skin should become burned, keep the burned areas covered with loose clothing. An application of aloe vera gel seems to soothe quite effectively. Do not break blisters if they form as this can lead to infection. Keep the affected area clean.

TICK INVASIONS

The very thought of walking through a valley infested with ticks makes most people's skin crawl. Perhaps it is because of the way the tick attaches itself to its host and then drains blood from places where we would rather not have something alien nibbling on us. Over the years, ticks have attracted our attention with their disease-carrying capability, and have managed to scare us greatly. Perhaps we need to get the problem in better perspective.

When adventuring in tick country:

- Wear long pants tucked into your socks as well as long-sleeved shirts tucked securely into your pants and held with a belt.
- Wear clothing light in color to make it easier to spot ticks. Tightly woven fabrics make it more difficult for ticks to hang on.
- Perform tick checks regularly, especially around the waistline, knees, breasts, armpits, ears, and crotch. Get someone else to check you over. This is not a good time to be modest.

Insect repellents for the skin containing Deet (N, N-Diethyl-Meta Tolumide) are considered to be the most effective in repelling ticks. But DEET is nasty stuff: Heed the warnings about Deet, especially when used on children, in Appendix VII.

A permethrin repellent, sold under the product name Permanone, a tick-repellent spray, is designed to be applied directly to clothing, tents, sleeping bags, and any surface other than skin. It kills ticks (and mosquitoes) on contact. It lasts up to 14 days and won't wash off in water.

If you find a tick imbedded in you or your child, get as close as possible to the head, and slowly pull the tick away from the skin without twisting or jerking. Sawyer's Tick Plier is recommended by a number of experts because it allows the user to slide the jaws beneath the body and extract the tick without squeezing the tick's body or cutting the tick. If it becomes too difficult to remove the tick by pulling, try applying a heavy mineral oil directly to the upper and lower surfaces of the tick. Wait 15 minutes and then try pulling the tick out again. The application of mineral oil clogs the breathing of the tick and serves to relax the tick's grip, making it easier to remove.

Wash the bite area with soap and water, and apply an antiseptic to the wound. Try to identify the tick. If it is a Lone Star or deer tick, place it in a vial or bag with a cotton swab of alcohol to preserve it for analysis in case disease symptoms appear.

The two most common tick-borne diseases in the West are Lyme disease and Rocky Mountain Spotted Fever. Rocky Mountain fever occurs in all parts of the United States, but is most common in the Appalachian region. The symptoms include headache, fever, severe muscle ache, and a rash on the palms of the hands and the soles of the feet that spreads to other parts of the body. It needs to be treated with antibiotics.

Lyme disease has occurred in every state except Alaska and Hawaii. Its symptoms include fever, headache, chills, fatigue, a volcano-shaped welt where the tick was attached, soreness, and swelling, most significantly in the joint areas. It needs to be treated with antibiotics.

Medicines and Drugs

PAIN-RELIEF DRUGS

Do not administer any of the following listed drugs to a child without the express guidance and direction of a medical doctor.

Aspirin: Mild analgesic, anti-inflammatory, fever-reducing. Interferes with blood clotting, can cause nausea. Don't give to children.

Motrin: Anti-inflammatory and moderate pain relief. May cause stomach irritation and nausea.

Tylenol: For relief of minor to moderate pain such as muscle ache and inflammation. May cause liver damage if overdosed. This drug is used as primary pain relief in many first-aid kits.

Tylenol with codeine (narcotic, prescription only): For pain and reduction of fever. Codeine sometimes causes nausea, constipation, and possible allergic reaction.

Lidocaine gel 2 percent (prescription only): Topical pain relief and local anesthetic.

ALLERGIC-REACTION DRUGS

Benadryl: Acts as an antihistamine, sedative, and anti-itch treatment. Use with caution, may cause drowsiness, constipation, weakness, headache, difficulty in urination, and diarrhea.

Ana-Kit: Injection of epinephrine and Chlo-Amine tablets to relieve severe allergic reaction. May cause headache, anxiety, or heart palpitations.

Caladryl lotion: A calamine and Benadryl lotion to relieve minor skin irritations.

Hydrocortisone ointment 25 percent: Steroid ointment for more severe skin reactions.

GASTROINTESTINAL DRUGS

Lomotil: To control diarrhea. Use only if the diarrhea compromises safety or an ability to travel. It is possible to introduce serious infection and start a fever because of bowel retention.

Maalox: Neutralizes stomach acids and relieves indigestion. Can produce mild diarrhea.

Seams don't stay sealed forever. Check your tent seams periodically to be sure they are still waterproof.

ANTIBIOTIC DRUGS

You must know what infection you are treating, otherwise the antibiotic is worthless. Broad-spectrum antibiotics are best, but you should always be aware of what specific type of infections will most likely be encountered.

Septra DS (prescription only): Urinary tract infections, diarrhea illness. May cause allergic reaction.
Keflex (prescription only): Skin infections, respiratory tract, urinary tract, inner-ear infection. May cause allergic reaction.
Neosporin ointment: Helps prevent infection in minor cuts and abrasions.

ANTISEPTICS

Betadine: For topical cleaning of the skin around the wound or before lancing a blister. If using to cleanse a wound, use 25 percent Betadine to 75 percent sterile water. Never use Betadine in a deep wound.

SKIN PREPARATION

Tincture of benzoin: Prepares skin for application of adhesive.

OTHER DRUGS TO CONSIDER

Cough suppressant: For example, Robitussin with codeine.
Decongestant: Such as Afrin nasal spray (not recommended for prolonged periods or for use at high altitudes), Sudafed, or Actifed.
Antibiotic eye drops: For example, Neosporin ophthalmic drops.

Skin care: For example, Vitamin A + D Ointment, which soothes rashes and dry skin.

BANDAGES, DRESSINGS, AND OTHER ITEMS

Sterile gauze pads: A variety of 2-inch by 2-inch and 4-inch by 4-inch pads.

Roller gauze: Kling or Kerlex.

Non-stick dressings: Telfa pads (coat with antibacterial ointment and petroleum, but change frequently to prevent drying out and adhering to the skin).

Inch-wide adhesive tape.

Butterfly bandages or Steristrips assortment.

Ace Wrap: Three-inch-wide bandage.

Large compress: Use sanitary napkins.

Band-Aids: An assortment of cloth bandages. I also recommend carrying some Snoopy Strips, as children seem to love them.

Moleskin: For the prevention and treatment of friction sores and blisters.

SecondSkin: To cover blisters, although I have known it to stick to the wound and create a painful and difficult removal.

Triangular bandage: To hold dressings in place, attach splints, and create slings.

EQUIPMENT AND ACCESSORIES

Tweezers

Needle

Single-sided razor blade

Bandage scissors

Irrigation syringe

Low-reading thermometer

SAM splint or wire mesh

Space blanket

Waterproof matches
Emergency report form
Pencil
Emergency contact numbers
Money for a phone call
Snakebite kit (Sawyer kit)
Dental kit: oil of cloves, cotton pads, and wax

SPECIFICALLY FOR KIDS

Dr. Barbara Kennedy, a pediatrician, National Outdoor Leadership School graduate, member of the Wilderness Medical Society, mother of four, and author of Adventure Medical Kits' *A Medical Guide to Traveling With Children,* offers the following medical tips for families experiencing the wilderness with children:

- Standard first-aid kits carried by families must be adapted to meet infants' and children's special needs. Actual items carried will vary depending on the ages of the children, preexisting medical conditions, length of travel, specific environment traveled in, and the first-aid knowledge of the parents.
- Infants can develop infections and become hypothermic, hyperthermic, and dehydrated more rapidly than adults or older children. Carry a digital thermometer and the appropriate lubricant for monitoring rectal temperatures. Temperatures of 100°F and over require immediate medical attention in a child younger than 4 months of age. A bulb syringe is also useful, not only because it can be used to suck mucus from the throat and nasal passages of infants, but also because it may be used to flush foreign bodies from ears and administer enemas.
- Blisters bother children of all ages. Feet should receive attention the minute friction or irritation is noticed. Always leave blisters intact unless infection is suspected. A fluid, gel-laminate

(SecondSkin) and an adhesive pad are very effective in the prevention and treatment of blisters.

- Most children under 5 cannot swallow pills. Chewable medications are preferred. If chewable medicine is not available, liquid medicine will work, but it adds weight and containers can leak. Most children can chew tablets once their first molars are present—usually around 15 months. For children who cannot chew, chewable medications may be crushed between spoons and mixed with food.
- Reduction of weight and bulk is a primary concern in any first-aid kit. One way to do that is to select medications and items that have multiple uses. For example, Desitin, best known for helping to prevent diaper rash, is also an excellent sunblock because 40 percent of it is zinc oxide.

CHAPTER 10

Teaching Children to Survive

FEAR AND PANIC ARE THE GREATEST DANGERS TO ANY HUMAN being in the outdoors. While it is true that natural acts and other unforeseeable circumstances claim injuries and lives each year, most deaths and injuries can be prevented by staying calm and thinking through the situation. Staying calm is not so easy to do, however, if you have little knowledge or information on which to base your decisions. This is why it is so important to teach your children basic wilderness skills that will help them in an emergency. Teach them how to "stay found," how to build a fire, how to look for shelter, where to find water, and other basic survival skills.

This is not the place for a vast treatise on survival skills for children. There are already a number of good books on the subject. The aim of this chapter is to point out the very basic information you need to teach your children, so they will feel comfortable and safe—even in stressful situations.

The Art of Knowing Where You Are

It has been said of Daniel Boone that when asked if he was ever lost his reply was, "Disoriented for a couple of days, maybe. Lost, never." The major difference between Boone and the majority of weekend wilderness explorers is one of skill. Boone could always hunt, trap, find water, build a shelter, make a boat, and gradually find his way out of a predicament. The average family, however, has neither the skill to survive off the land nor the time to spend wandering.

It is important for parents to realize that anyone can get lost. All it takes is a dense mist, a few unplanned turns in the woods, nightfall, or a storm to disorient most people outdoors. I have seen people who swore up and down that they had infallible senses of direction get utterly lost after I led them on short, albeit circuitous, hikes away from camp.

A good sense of direction comes from keeping your senses wide open to all sources of information: sights, sounds, smells, and even touch. Teach your children to be aware of significant landmarks such as tall trees, prominent rocks, or large meadows. Teach them also to look all around them, to make a mental map of what is in the front, at the sides, and at the back—and how perspectives change. Quite often, a tree that looked unique and significant in one direction, looks completely different when viewed from another.

Sounds such as a river, a car on a road, or a foghorn on a lighthouse, are also important bits of information. Don't overlook the smell and feel of an area. A valley may feel damp and smell a certain way. Water can quite often be smelled from a distance. Individually, each of the senses contains a fragment of information to help you and your children to stay "found"—that is, to know where you are in relation to known landmarks. Only if you can combine all the fragments of information into careful and complete observation can you begin to create that mythical "good sense of direction."

Many of us have heard it hundreds of times, but I am going to say it again: "Plan your hike and hike your plan." Good planning goes far toward ensuring a safe trip. Teach your children about the area you are visiting, too. Most children will

It is most often better to take 100 steps around an obstacle than 10 steps over it.

find topo maps confusing and impossible to understand. Try, instead, to draw a special map for your children. Show them major landmarks, where the roads are, how the trail looks, where the water sources are, where you plan to camp, and where some of the nearby towns are.

A child should never leave camp alone under any circumstances. In addition, no one should ever leave home or camp without telling someone responsible where they are going. This applies to adults and children. There are no exceptions to these rules and they must become a hard-and-fast law for your family.

Younger children have a habit of wandering off without realizing where they are going. Getting sidetracked is a young child's mission in life, it seems. After wandering from one little adventure to another, a child can suddenly look around and discover that nothing looks familiar. Because of this, you must watch your children very closely. I recommend that all the children in your family know their home address, phone number, parents' names, and campsite number where applicable. If a child has trouble remembering all this, write it down and have them carry it with them in a safe place, or wear it like a name tag.

Children of all ages should carry a whistle. The sound of a whistle is much more easily heard and more energy efficient than a tiny voice screaming for help. Teach your children to blow the whistle loudly and distinctly in sets of three: *tweet—tweet—tweet.* This is a signal for help, and help will arrive if anyone is within earshot. It's a great temptation for a child to blow on the whistle at all times, so you must teach them to use it only in an emergency.

Children should gradually and very patiently be taught visual navigation without the aid of a map. In other words, how to get from point A to point B and then back to point A again. This is done by continually observing and remembering prominent landmarks or features of the terrain they are traveling through. You will have to encourage them to take time to make a mental map every so often until this becomes an unconscious or natural thing for them. As children grow older and show an aptitude for, and interest in, map reading, then add that to their arsenal of wilderness skills. The way to teach children to observe distant and nearby landmarks and features is to stop frequently and have them name things that stand out to them. At each subsequent stop, ask your children to remember and recite each landmark and feature they have selected up until this point. Your children should be looking for things such as distant peaks, far-off ridges, a towering grove of trees that stands separate and above the rest, the distinct shape of a meadow, a strangely shaped tree or bush, a cave, a stream, and so on. When you head back that way, take the time to sit down with your children and challenge them to remember what it is they will be looking for. Help them remember the landmarks if necessary. Then, put your children in charge as they navigate from recognizable landmark to recognizable landmark all the way back to home or camp. Remember to be very patient and loving. Initially, and especially if they are very young, children are apt to forget things and get somewhat distracted.

Lost Children

"I'm lost!" That initial moment of panic surges through the human mind like a runaway train. If the panic is not controlled, the body soon follows the mind's lead, often taking off, plowing through bushes, trees, and meadows in a desperate effort to find something familiar. This type of panic is common and can lead to complete exhaustion, dehydration, injury, and even death.

Your children must be taught to sit down and think quietly if they become lost. When they panic and begin frantically to try to find their way back to camp, they usually get into deeper trouble. If your children are taught to sit down and think carefully, a solution usually becomes evident. Teach them to look around painstakingly, retracing their steps in their mind. Very often, after some calm thinking, the trail home can be discovered.

Sometimes, however, the way back to camp is not evident at all, and your child may feel a need to get up and explore the surrounding area in search of a trail. This is okay if the child can accurately mark the area in which he or she is now standing and can return to it after the initial search. If a child can remember clearly the way back to camp, he or she should proceed as long as everything continues to look familiar. It is critical for your children to understand the importance of staying in one place if they have no idea where they are. Wandering children make for extremely difficult rescues.

If the child is confident about again finding the point where he or she sat down, he or she can begin working outward in a circular pattern until a familiar piece of ground or terrain is discovered. While working their way out in this cir-

Setting up camp under a tree with limbs that may fall, or near rocks that may tumble, is asking for a lump on the head, or worse.

cular fashion, it is important for your children always to keep their original starting position in sight.

From each familiar point that is discovered, your children should be taught to find another landmark that now identifies this area, and repeat the process. Essentially, your children are moving from familiar point to familiar point and marking their progress along the way. Once the children discover a trail or road that is recognizable, they can then head out in a straight line toward home or help.

It may appear strange to mention molestation in the context of what to do if a child is lost, but it is an important consideration. Children are sometimes molested, and come to harm, often when they are perceived to be helpless. It is vital that you teach your children not to run thankfully into the arms of a stranger who seems to be offering help. Give your children some idea about who can be trusted and who cannot, so they can make an informed decision for themselves. When she was much younger, I taught my daughter to trust a police officer or a ranger, and adults in groups. Individual men offering help were immediately suspect. It sickened me to have to teach her not to trust, but with the rising rate of abductions and molestations I felt I had no choice.

FINDING SHELTER

If a child is really lost and has no idea in which direction home or camp lies, finding shelter is the most important survival skill to master. Although there are usually small caves, deadfalls, hollow logs, eroded overhangs, and other natural shelters that appear to offer good shelter, they often do not live up to their promise in bad weather. At best, natural enclosures usually provide only temporary refuge, and at worst may become death traps.

Teach your child the criteria for judging an adequate shelter. It must:

- protect you from wind
- retain your body heat
- protect you from rain and snow

Wind protection is extremely important. A strong wind coupled with rain can cause a rapid loss of body heat. This leads to hypothermia and death, even when the air temperature is 50°F. Wind also rapidly increases the rate of dehydration. Luckily, wind protection is the easiest to find: almost anything—a fallen log, a dense bush, or a large rock—will break the wind.

Protection against rain or snow is more difficult to find because now you now need shelter from above as well as from the sides. Dense bushes, thick brush piles, downed trees, natural caves, and large rock piles are all possibilities for good shelter from snow and rain.

Unfortunately, most natural shelters do not provide the other important criterion for a shelter: heat retention. If you and your children study the way animals construct their burrows or nests, you'll notice that they hollow out an area in a tree or the ground and then line it, or stuff it, with leaves, grasses, twigs, and even fur. Teach your children to do the same with dead leaves, twigs, and grasses, to help them stay warm.

As I said, natural shelters can be dangerous, and your children must be taught to identify the dangers. Deadfalls, rock piles, and caves are all potential homes for animals and insects. Take care not to suddenly disturb a nest of bees, a poisonous snake, or a bear. Perhaps even more dangerous is the possibility that the natural shelter could collapse, trapping your child inside. Teach your children to be very cautious around deadfalls. Where one tree has fallen, more may be ready to tumble.

One thing to remember about a natural shelter is that it is well camouflaged. I can vividly recall one particular rescue, when I was actively involved in search-and-rescue missions,

If you are cold, even in a sleeping bag, try putting on a hat.

where we were looking for an elderly man who had been missing for several days. It had snowed heavily, covering up all previous signs and making it difficult for the dogs to find any scent. All we had to go on was instinct and educated guesses based upon the lie of the land and our deductions as to how the man would have traveled.

We swept the area for several days, back and forth, covering every inch with what we thought was a fine-toothed comb. But we found no sign of him, and were forced to give up. Later that month, after the snow had melted, a man hiking in that area stumbled across the man's pack near a downed tree. Looking further, he found the man huddled inside the trunk with branches pulled in front of the opening to protect him from the snow. He had frozen to death, and we had walked back and forth in front of that tree on several occasions without realizing he was in there. After that particular search, I recommended that anyone using a natural shelter leave some sign outside to alert rescuers. The sign should be obvious and visible enough that it will not get obscured by snow or debris falling on the ground.

A specially constructed shelter provides perhaps the best means of staying warm, dry, and secure, and it will stand out from the surrounding environment. While many survival books teach you to build lean-tos, A-frames, igloos, and even cabins, the quickest and most efficient shelter to build is one I was taught about when I learned Indian lore. It uses only material from the forest floor and requires no tools. A child can construct this shelter in about an hour and a half.

Pick an area that has good drainage, one that will neither

> An emergency or survival situation is the only time to forget about the rules of minimizing impact on the environment. Build a signal fire, draw attention to yourself, and do everything you can to stay alive.

be washed away nor buried under a falling tree or an avalanche of rocks. Also make absolutely certain that your chosen area is not over an animal hole, an ants' nest, or a thicket of poison oak, ivy, or sumac.

Find a large rock, stump, log, or other support. I was taught to use a log or downed tree as one wall, but downed trees with trunks large enough are not always present. Ideally, the log or rock support should be about 3 feet high. Find a large stick, several inches in diameter and about 5 feet long—or longer, if the shelter is for someone taller than 5 feet. Lean one end of the stick on the rock, log, or stump and let the other end rest on the ground to form a ridgepole.

Collect a large number of smaller sticks to lean upright against each side of the ridgepole, creating an upside down V-frame for your shelter. Leave an opening at the front on one side, facing away from the wind.

Now your child should crawl inside the shelter to make sure there is enough room to lie down comfortably without disturbing the side walls.

Next, pile twigs, lots of dried leaves, and small branches on top of the framework you have built. Make this a generous layer of leaves and twigs, about 2 to 3 feet thick.

Then place a snug layer of small branches and twigs on top, heavy enough to hold everything in place, even in a strong wind. But don't make it so heavy that it crushes or compresses the leaves and twigs making up the inner lining. The air spaces make good insulation.

Finally, stuff the inside of the shelter full of dried leaves, pine needles, ferns, and so on, so the interior is loosely filled from top to bottom. With the shelter now complete, all your child has to do is squirm and snuggle inside feet-first. This type of shelter will keep a child or adult warm and dry for days, even in the worst conditions.

FINDING WATER

When you are lost, finding water is second only to finding shelter in the scale of importance for survival. Dehydration is a killer. Your children should know that a person can survive for a very long time with a good shelter and a supply of water, even if there is no food.

Water can be found or distilled. The easiest way to get water is to discover a stream or a source of moving water. Moving water is the least likely to be polluted. Tree stumps, potholes, and stagnant ponds are other water sources, but they are likely to be dangerously polluted. Sometimes you can find water by digging a hole in the damp bed of a stream.

You can even get moisture from dew-soaked leaves and grasses. Instead of crawling around licking the leaves, soak up moisture with a cotton cloth, then squeeze out the water into your mouth. As a last resort, you can collect water in a still. More of that later.

But your children also need to be wary of the water they find. Most water is polluted to some degree, and the pollutants

Wilderness navigation is a 360-degree effort.

When you are trying to conserve water, cut out caffeine and alcohol. Both are diuretics that remove valuable water from your system.

N

can turn a very basic survival situation into a critical emergency. For this reason, water must be treated or purified.

There are several ways to treat water. Boiling it is the best guarantee of purification. If your child possesses a pot or cup, and can make a fire, boiling the water for 5 to 6 minutes will make it safe to drink. At least, it will destroy all biological pollutants.

In a survival situation, filtering the water is not the complete answer. It's unlikely that a lost kid will be carrying a commercial filter. But sometimes filtering is better than nothing. To filter very muddy water, or water filled with debris, pour it through a bandanna or an article of cotton clothing.

Chemical purification works very well to remove biological impurities, but it does not touch the chemical pollutants. Products made of iodine, such as Potable Aqua or Polar Pure, are easily used, effective chemical treatments. Teach your child how to use them and include a bottle of Potable Aqua in your child's compact survival kit.

DISTILLING WATER

A homemade solar still could save your child's life. It requires only a large piece of thin plastic sheet, a cup, and a length of plastic tubing. It's a very useful skill to know about, and the water it collects is pure.

Find some ground that feels damper than the rest, maybe the bed of a stream or the bottom of a gully, maybe a place where the plant life is greener and more abundant. The area should be open to the sun and sky, not deeply shaded.

Dig a hole about 2 feet deep and 3 feet across. Place a cup

Learn some basic search-and-rescue skills.

Wool will keep you warm when wet; but it stinks, becomes heavy, and itches. If you have a choice, select synthetics such as Polartec.

at the bottom of the hole in the center, and put one end of the plastic tube in the bottom of the cup. If the dirt you are digging is dry, and it doesn't look as though you can squeeze any moisture out of it, fill it with green leaves, and urinate in it. You can even add unboiled, untreated water, because the solar distillation process will leave pollutants behind.

Cover the hole with the clear plastic sheet, heaping dirt around the edges to keep it in place and stop moisture escaping.

Finally, place a rock or other small weight in the center of the plastic sheet so the plastic sheet forms a cone with its point directly above the cup. The plastic tube should lead from the cup, up and out to one side of the plastic cone without touching it.

The sun, even on a hazy or partly cloudy day, will warm the soil and cause moisture to evaporate and condense on the underside of the plastic. Droplets will roll down the inside of the plastic and drip off the point of the cone into the cup. Your child will be able to drink out of the cup by sucking on the outside end of the plastic tube. This method works well and, as I said, provides safe water even from urine or dirty water, but it is slow. Teach your children to be patient. They may need to move the still if it dries out the area and production slows down. For a long stay, three or four such stills would be good to have working, but one, used wisely, will keep a person alive.

When you teach your children about water, you have an excellent opportunity to inform them about environmental

Pita bread and tortillas make great camping food. They stay fresh for as long as 10 days.

pollution. Explain to them that until quite recently, most wilderness water was pure. Not so long ago, humans could drink directly from many streams and rivers, but now people dump garbage, human waste, and chemicals into our water sources. Thus, every drop of water on the face of the earth is becoming polluted. Perhaps this will get them to think about their impact upon the earth.

BUILDING FIRES

Knowing how to build a fire is an important survival skill. It ranks right behind knowing how to build a shelter and how to find water. A fire may be needed for water purification, warmth, cooking, and even signaling.

The most important thing to teach all children about fire is respect. It is a dangerous tool. The smallest flame is capable of growing into a raging fire that can destroy vast amounts of land and many animals.

Not all children should be allowed to build fires, but it's a very individual decision. There is no hard-and-fast rule about what age is appropriate. For example, I was building fires from scratch at age 8, yet I had several friends who should not have been trusted with a match until age 18—and there was even some doubt about that.

Most simply put, the teaching process begins with your child helping you to collect wood and watching you build and maintain a fire. Children will soon learn where to find the driest wood, how to find dry kindling under logs or around the base of a pine tree, and what type and shape of wood is best for kindling and feeding the fire. They will also learn when to break the rules about not taking dead branches and twigs from trees, and, in very wet conditions, when a fire is necessary for survival. Teach your children to avoid poison oak, poison ivy, and poison sumac because inhaling the smoke from any of these poisonous plants is very irritating to the skin, eyes, and lungs, and can often be dangerous.

As your children become proficient at collecting and gathering the right kind of wood, they can begin helping to maintain the fire. This will teach them how to create a proper bed of coals for cooking, how to keep the flames from getting too hot, how to put wood into the flames safely to feed them, and how best to put out a fire.

Once children have shown they can reliably gather wood and maintain the flame, it is time for them to learn firebuilding from scratch. You might think of some appropriate award when your children reach this honored position, to give them a feeling for the importance of this task. "Lord of the Firebuilders" or "Honored Member of the Fire Clan" are two of my favorites.

Teach your children to select a fire site that is free from ground debris, roots, and other vegetation that might catch fire and spread the flame to surrounding trees. Also, the fire should not be built under overhanging tree limbs or within 10 to 15 feet of any shelter.

Beware of building a fire in a cave or next to damp rocks. Moisture in the rocks can reach boiling point, expand, and explode the rock like a bomb. When I was 10 years old, a mem-

N W E S

Don't go anywhere without the 10 essentials:
flashlight, map, compass, extra food, extra clothing, sunglasses, first-aid supplies, pocket knife, waterproof matches, fire starter.

ber of our campfire group tossed a wet sandstone rock into the fire. It exploded and sent embers showering over all of us. Fortunately no one was hurt, but the potential for serious injury was very high.

Show children how to pick an area with natural windbreaks and how to clear the area of all loose debris. Teach them to dig into the dirt, creating a shallow depression about 6 to 12 inches deep and 2 to 2½ feet across. Encircle the depression with rocks to help contain the fire. Finally, make a heat reflector and windbreak on the windward side of the fire ring. The windbreak should be in the shape of a half circle and provide an adequate shield against the wind. It should also provide a surface to reflect the fire's heat toward persons sitting by the fire.

Once the fire site has been safely prepared, the children need to gather plenty of kindling and enough wood to last the night comfortably. Beginning with the kindling, bunch up a ball of frayed bark, dried grasses, and tiny twigs from a pine tree, evergreen, or other available tree. Now, lay very small twigs and sticks, not much larger than the kindling, up against one another and over the ball, forming a tepee shape. Leave a small opening through which you can later shove a flaming match to ignite the fire. Continue adding more wood, gradually longer and thicker, up to the width of two fingers. Maintain the tepee shape at all times. Once the fire is built to satisfaction, a match is carefully struck, shielded from the wind, and placed next to the waiting ball of kindling to ignite it.

The tepee fire is the very best fire for quick lighting, even in severe weather. It will put out a tremendous amount of heat, even with a relatively small fire, and is quite easy to maintain. When adding wood, lay each piece carefully into the flame and always keep the shape of the tepee intact. Instruct your children not to toss wood on a fire any old how, as at best it sends up a shower of sparks, and at worst it could destroy the fire.

SURVIVAL TACTICS

One of the best ways to teach your children to survive in the wilderness is to simulate survival situations during overnight camp-outs. I remember that when I learned to make a shelter, build a fire, and search for food, there was an air of adventure about it. We were learning about Indian lore, reading their stories, dancing their dances, studying animals, and using our imaginations to the maximum. We even became a special clan and lived out in the woods for a while.

It was in this atmosphere of mystery and adventure that we made our fires, built our shelters, and searched for water. Sure, we weren't becoming hardened survivalists (we were given three waterproofed matches with which to build a fire, and camp was only a mile away), but we were taught to use our heads, not panic, and feel comfortable in the outdoors.

Your children will learn much about the land and themselves if an air of mystery and adventure is created for them. Become explorers for a weekend, form your own Indian clan, or pretend to be hibernating bears, anything to create a mood for fun and learning together. Take all your camping gear with you to a local park, campground, or even your own backyard, but don't use your tent, stove, or sleeping bag unless you have to. Build your own shelters and sleep in them, make a fire and cook with it, distill water and drink it. Most of all, have fun—and see how your children will learn.

Foiling the Criminals

Although it pains me to say this, criminals have discovered that parking areas and campgrounds are a great source of wealth and easily duped victims. Who, after all, expects to get robbed, raped, or mugged in a park?

Park rangers and law-enforcement officials all agree, however, that with a little forethought and common sense, most criminals can be stopped in their tracks. Here are their suggestions:

- Never leave a wallet or anything valuable locked in your car. Take it with you or leave it at home. I tuck my driver's license, credit card and money into a special waterproof nylon pouch I take with me. I leave my urban wallet at home.
- Ask rangers if the trailhead where you are planning to leave your car has a high incidence of break-ins. If so, try to choose another parking place. I have often parked my car at a garage in a nearby town and been driven to and from the trailhead for a small fee. You'll have to negotiate that, depending on distance.
- Never wander trails alone, now matter how short they are. That is especially true for children and young teenagers.
- Always travel in pairs around a campground. No one goes to the bathrooms by themselves.
- Report suspicious activity to rangers.
- Never stay in an urban park after dark.
- Sign in at all trailheads, even if you are just going for a day hike.
- If you have the choice, use your older vehicle for the outing. A brand-new car announces very loudly that valuables are available for stealing. If your only car is new, be sure your insurance will cover vandalism.
- Always try to leave your car at parking areas where lots of people are coming and going throughout the day.
- If the parking site is littered with broken windshield glass, assume cars have been broken into there before. Move on.
- Never leave car keys hidden on the vehicle. There are few options for hiding a key and you can be assured the crooks know them all.
- Don't leave a note on your dashboard saying where you will be going and when you will be back. Such advice is often given, but I would refrain from it. Although it helps the

search party if you get into trouble, it also makes things easier for car burglars.

- Always park with your trunk or hatch facing the main parking lot, not the woods. No sense in giving the criminal element privacy.

Tips in a Nutshell

1. Teach children to sweep their eyes through 360 degrees as they walk. Remember important and easy-to-recognize landmarks that help find the way home later. Use your eyes, ears, and nose to help determine where camp is.
2. Never leave camp alone.
3. Create special hand-drawn maps for children to use, featuring major landmarks, roads, trails, water sources, camp, and nearby towns. Show them how to use the map.
4. Teach your children how and when to use the whistle around their necks. Three distinct blasts indicate trouble.
5. Teach your children to sit and think quietly if they get lost. Panic will only make things worse. If they remember clearly the way back to camp, they should proceed as long as everything continues to look familiar. Otherwise, they must stay put.
6. If lost, find or build a shelter first. A shelter made of sticks and debris is very effective and quite warm. A child can survive in this type of shelter many days even in severe weather.
7. Finding water is the second essential. Show your child how to get water.
8. Making a fire is the third priority. Fires are important for warmth and for signaling.
9. Last on the list is finding food. With shelter and water, a child can survive for many days, even if no food is available. Teach your children not to eat plants unless they are certain they are not poisonous.

APPENDIX I

Family Adventuring Checklist

HERE IS A CHECKLIST TO AID YOU IN PLANNING YOUR NEXT FAMILY adventure. Not all the items will apply to every trip. Pack only what you need and leave the rest at home—remember, you've got to carry what you pack.

PACKS

Backpack (external or internal frame)
Waterproof pack cover
Child carrier
Day pack or fanny pack

SHELTER

Lightweight tent (including poles, stakes, and guy lines)
Mosquito netting (for your head when sleeping under the stars)
Nylon tarp, 9 feet x 12 feet, with grommets

SLEEPING

Sleeping bag (down or synthetic)
Sleeping pad
Pillow
Ground cloth

TEN-PLUS ESSENTIALS

Sunglasses
Water bottle
Nylon cord (50 feet)
Waterproof/windproof matches
Flashlight (extra bulb and batteries)
Fire starter
Pocket knife or multitool

Toilet paper
Topographic map
Compass
Emergency blanket
Whistle
Signal mirror
Emergency snacks

KITCHEN

Stove
Fuel
Primer paste
Lighter or matches
Windscreen
Cookset
Frying pan
Water bag (collapsible)
Storage containers for food
Ziploc Bags (freezer weight)
Large spoon
Knife
Spatula
Can opener (GI folding type)
Small whisk
Small grater
Pot grips
Knife, fork, spoon
Plate
Cup
Bowl
Cutting board (small nylon kind)
Ice chest
Scrub pads
Biodegradable soap
Paper towels
Aluminum foil
Spice kit

FIRST-AID KIT

(See Chapter 10)

TOILETRIES

Comb or brush
Toothbrush and toothpaste
Dental floss
Deodorant
Small towel
Shaving kit
Biodegradable skin and hair soap
Moisturizing lotion
Towlettes
Sunscreen (25 SPF or better)
Lip balm
Tampons

CLOTHING

First layer:
Underwear
Long underwear (tops and bottoms)
Liner socks
Wool outer socks
T-shirt

Second layer:
Wool shirt
Polartec, fleece, or wool sweater
Shorts
Long pants

Protective layer:
Wool or synthetic hat
Sun hat
Bunting or Polartec or fleece jacket
Parka (synthetic or down)
Wool mittens
Rainsuit (jacket and pants)
Gaitors
Windbreaker
Hiking boots
Camp shoes or sneakers

MISCELLANEOUS GEAR

Butane lantern or candle lantern
Fishing gear and fishing license
Trowel
Thermometer
Bandanna
Note pad and pencil
Camera, film, lenses
Binoculars
Plastic trash bags

FUN AND GAMES

Frisbee
Nerf ball
Hacky Sack
Cards
Miniature games (backgammon, checkers, chess)
Harmonica
Kazoo
Paperback books
Coloring books
Star guide
Mini microscope
Magnifying glass
Small plastic collection containers
Aquarium net
Sketch pad
Pencils
Crayons
Colored felt-tip pens
Gold pan and mineral book

BIKE TOURING AND MOUNTAIN BIKING

Cycling shorts
Cycling gloves
Cycling shoes
Helmet
Patch kit
Spare parts
Mini tool kit

CROSS-COUNTRY SKIING

Waxless skis
Boots
Bindings
Poles
Extra ski tip
Basic repair parts

PADDLING

Canoe or kayak
Paddles
Life jackets
Waterproof duffel bags
Waterproof containers for camera gear
Rope to secure duffels and contents in boat.

GEAR FOR INFANTS

Bottles and extra nipples
Rubber or plastic pants
Diapers
Sleep suits
Extra clothing
Warm snuggle suit
Rain suit
Baby food
Baby wipes
Baby powder or corn starch

APPENDIX II

Recommended Reading

MAGAZINES

Backpacker, 610-967-5171
Outside, 505-989-7100
Bicycling, 610-967-5171
Canoe & Kayak, 800-692-2663, 425-827-6363
Family Fun, 800-289-4849

BOOKS

If you can't find any of the following books or other related books in your local bookstore, don't despair. Some of these titles may be out of print, in which case you might have to consult your library or second-hand bookstore. There are several excellent mail-order bookstores, including these on the Web:

www.amazon.com
Adventurous Traveler Book store:
www.adventuroustraveler.com

Here is a list of titles you will find interesting and informative:

Axcell, Claudia, Diana Cooke, and Vikki Kinmont. *Simple Foods for the Pack.* San Francisco: Sierra Club Books, 1986.

Barker, Harriett. *Supermarket Backpacker.* New York: Contemporary Books, 1978.

Bowden, Marcia. *Nature for the Very Young.* New York: John Wiley & Sons, Inc., 1989.

Brown, Tom, Jr. *Tom Brown's Field Guide to Nature and Survival for Children.* New York: Berkley Publishing Group, 1989.

Carline, Jan D., et al. *Mountaineering First Aid.* Seattle: The Mountaineers, 1996.

Cornell, Joseph. *Sharing Nature with Children.* Nevada City, CA: Dawn Publications, 1979.

Harrison, David, and Judy Harrison. *Canoe Tripping with Children.* Old Saybrook, CT: ICS/Globe Pequot, 1990.

Hodgson, Michael. *Compass and Map Navigator.* Old Saybrook, CT: ICS/Globe Pequot, 1996.

Logue, Victoria, Frank Logue, and Mark Carroll. *Kids Outdoors.* Camden, ME: Ragged Mountain Press, 1996.

Long, John, and Michael Hodgson. *The Dayhiker's Handbook.* Camden, ME: Ragged Mountain Press, 1996.

McCairen, Pat. *River Runner's Recipes.* Birmingham, AL: Menasha Ridge Press, 1994.

Sheperdson, Carl. *The Family Canoe Trip.* Harrisburg, PA: Stackpole Books, 1985.

Simer, Peter, and John J. Sullivan. *The National Outdoor Leadership School's Wilderness Guide.* New York: Simon and Schuster, 1985.

APPENDIX III

Organizations

ORGANIZATIONS

American Canoe Association, 703-451-0141; http://www.aca-paddler.org
American Hiking Society, 301-565-6704; http://www.orca.org/ahs/
American Red Cross, 202-737-8300
Appalachian Mountain Club, 617-523-0636
International Mountain Biking Association, 303-545-9011; http://www.imba.com
League of American Bicylists, 202-822-1333
National Audubon Society, 212-979-3000
National Parks and Conservation Association, 800-628-7275; http://www.npca.org
The Nature Conservancy, 703-841-5300
Sharing Nature Foundation, 530-478-7650
Sierra Club, 415-977-5500; http://www.sierraclub.org
Wilderness Medicine Institute, 970-641-3572

APPENDIX IV

Cyberhiking

THE INTERNET IS EXPLODING WITH COMPANIES OFFERING SERVICES, information, and entertainment. I have put together a list of some of the best sites that I could recommend to you at the time of publication. To contact them you will need access to the Internet. Once in the front door through a netserver, enter the Uniform Resource Locator (URL) code given below, and your computer will take you "cyberhiking." Enjoy, but don't get too lost in the electronic world . . . there's a real world waiting for you right outside your door.

Adventurous Traveler Bookstore, http://www.adventuroustraveler.com or http://www.gorp.com/atbook.htm

American Discovery Trail, http://www.teleport.com/~walking/adt.htm

American Hiking Society information pages, http://www.teleport.com/~walking/ahs.htm

Appalachian Mountain Club Home Page, http://www.lehigh.edu/ludas/public/www-data/amc.html

Australia Bushwalker's Page, http://www.anatomy.su.oz.au/danny/bushwalking/

Bureau of Land Management, http://www.blm.gov

Canadian Parks Banff National Park (this entry leads to other site access), http://www.worldweb.com/ParksCanada-Banff/

DeLorme Map Company, http://www.delorme.com

GORP (Great Outdoor Recreation Page), http://www.gorp.com/

Hiking and Walking Home Page, http://www.teleport.com/~walking/hiking.html

Michael Hodgson's Adventure Network, http://www.adventurenetwork.com

Hosteling Information Page, http://www.hostels.com/hostels/

Leave No Trace information pages by NOLS, http://www.lnt.org

Maps Unlimited, http://wae.com/px/newcom/homepage.htm

National Park Service, http://www.nps.gov/nps

New Zealand Hiking Information, http://www.gorp.com/gorp/location/newzeal/newzeala.htm

Orienteering and Rogaining Home Page, http://www2.aos.princeton.edu/rdslater/orienteering

Outside Magazine Guide to Hiking, http://Outside.starwave.com

Rocky Mountain Outfitters, http://www.omix.com/rmo/

Sierra Club Home Page, http.//www.sierraclub.org/index.html

Trails Illustrated Maps, http://www.trailsillustrated.com

U.S. Fish and Wildlife Service, http://www.fws.gov/

U.S. Forest Service, http://www.fs.fed.us/

U.S. Geological Survey (USGS) topographic maps, http://info.er.usgs.gov/

Volksmarch and Walking Event Index, http://www.winternet.com/~stachour/vm/index.html

Yahoo Outdoor Magazines Reference Page, http://www.yahoo.com/Entertainment/Outdoors/Magazines/

Yahoo Hiking Reference Page, http://www.yahoo.com/Entertainment/Outdoors/Hiking/

Equipment Suppliers

All the gear listed below is available through specialty mail-order companies or at your specialty outdoor store. Use the telephone numbers or Internet addresses to find a retail outlet near you.

MAIL-ORDER COMPANIES

After the Stork, 800-441-4775
Bike Nashbar, 800-627-4227; http://www.nashbar.com
The Boundary Waters Catalog, 800-223-6565; http://www.piragis.com
Campmor, 201-226-7667; http://www.campmor.com
Chinook Medical Gear, Inc., 800-766-1365
L.L. Bean, Inc., 800-341-4341; http://www.llbean.com
The Nature Company, 800-227-1114
Northwest River Supplies, 800-635-5202
Patagonia, 800-638-6464; http://www.patagonia.com
Recreational Equipment, Inc., 800-426-4840; http://www.rei.com

ADULT AND CHILDRENS' PACKS

Camp Trails, 607-779-2200
Dana Designs, 406-587-4188
Eagle Creek, 800-874-9925
JanSport, 800-552-6776
Lowe Alpine, 303-465-0522
Overland, 800-487-8851

Ultimate Direction, 800-426-7229

BICYCLE GEAR

Bell Helmets, 800-456-2355
Burley Design, 541-687-1644 (bike trailers)
Rhode Gear, 800-776-5677 (bike trailers and child seats)

CHILDREN'S DAYPACKS AND SMALL PACKS

Camp Trails, 607-779-2200
Kelty, 800-423-2320
Osprey, 970-882-2221
Tough Traveler, Ltd., 800-468-6844

CHILD CARRIERS

Gerry Baby Products, 303-457-0926
Kelty, 800-423-2320
Lafuma AFmerica, Inc., 800-514-4807
Snugli, 303-457-0926
Tough Traveler, Ltd., 800-468-6844

CROSS-COUNTRY SKI GEAR

Mountain Man, 406-587-0310 (ski touring sleds)
Ridge Runner Products, 800-373-8776 (ski touring sleds)

FIRST-AID KITS

Adventure Medical Kits, 800-324-3517
Atwater Carey, 800-359-1646
Outdoor Research, 800-421-2421; http://www.orgear.com
Sawyer, 800-356-7811

CLOTHING

First layer and long underwear:
Helly-Hansen Lifa, 800-435-5901
Lowe Powerstretch, 303-465-3706
Moonstone Bipolar, 800-390-3312
Patagonia Capilene, 800-336-9090
PolarMax (made by Longworth Industries), 800-552-8585

Wool socks:
SmartWool, 970-879-2913
Wigwam, 920-457-5551

Sport-specific socks:
ThorLo, 800-438-0209

T-shirts, cotton/synthetic:
Patagonia GoT, 800-336-9090
Sierra Designs RayTator, 510-597-0860

Long-sleeved shirts:
Ex Officio Baja Plus, 800-644-7303

Second layers:
The following companies make products manufactured with Malden's Polartec 100 or 200, Powerstretch, or Bipolar:

Kenyon, 401-792-3704
Lowe Alpine, 303-465-3706

Marmot, 707-544-4590
North Face, 800-447-2333

Clothing specially for kids. Nicole recommends:
Cherry Tree, 800-869-7742
Chuck Roast, 603-447-5492
Helly-Hansen, 800-435-5901
Jolly Tundra, 507-647-6000
Log House Designs, 603-694-3373
Patagonia, 800-638-6464
Wickers, 800-648-7024
Wigwam Mills, Inc., 800-558-7760
Wyoming Woolens, 307-733-2892

Shorts:
Ex Officio AmphiShort, 800-644-7303
Kavu, 800-419-5288

Long pants:
Ex Officio AmphiPant, 800-644-7303
RailRiders, 617-864-5969

Jackets—bunting, Polartec, or fleece:
Lowe, 303-465-3706
Marker, 801-972-0404
Mountain Hardwear, 510-559-6700
North Face, 800-447-2333
Patagonia, 800-336-9090
Sierra Designs, 510-597-0860

Insulated hats:
While I am very partial to my British military wool beret, there are times when I wouldn't think of heading outdoors without a fleece-lined bomber hat such as the Adventure 16 Bomber, 619-283-2362.

Sun hats:
Sequel, 970-385-4660, makes my favorite sun hat, one that resembles something a Foreign Legionnaire might wear and it's called the Desert Rhat. Their loose-fitting clothing line is also excellent hot-weather wear.

Baseball caps:
Kavu, 800-419-5288

Men's waterproof, breathable jackets:
Columbia's Monte Verde II, 800-547-8066
Lowe's MFS Tech, 303-465-3706
Marmot's Cervino, 707-544-4590
Mountain Hardwear's Stratus, 510-559-6700
Nike's Storm F.I.T., 800-344-6453

Women's waterproof, breathable jackets:
Granted, I don't wear women's jackets. I depend on some very reliable testers, including my daughter, Nicole, and my fianceé, Therese. Here are their recommendations:

Lowe's Alpine Flash, 303-465-3706
Marmot's Thunderlight, 707-544-4590

Moonstone's Advantage, 800-390-3312
Mountain Hardwear's Exposure, 510-559-6700
Sierra Design's Eiger, 510-597-0860
North Face's Kichatna, 800-447-2333

Water-resistant windbreakers:
Patagonia's Pneumatic, 800-336-9090
Pearl Izumi's Zephyr Attack, 800-877-7080
Sierra Designs' high-altitude anorak, 510-597-0860

Children's sleeping bags:
The Baby Bag Co., 207-829-5038
Cascade Designs, 800-531-9531
Kelty, 800-423-2320
Slumberjack, 800-233-6283

Walking staffs/hiking poles:
Leki Sport, 800-255-9982

Compasses:
Brunton, 800-443-4871
Silva (made by Johnson Worldwide), 800-572-8822

Water filters:
General Ecology, 800-441-8166
MSR, 800-877-9677
PUR, 800-845-7873
SweetWater (made by Cascade Designs), 800-557-9338

Hiking boots for rock scrambling:
Five Tennie, 909-798-4222
La Sportiva, 303-443-8710

Light to midweight hiking boots:
Adidas, 800-423-4327
Asolo, 800-892-2668
Montrail (formerly One Sport), 800-826-1598
Nike, 800-344-6453
Salomon, 800-225-6850
Tecnica, 603-298-8032
Vasque, 800-224-4453

Sun protection:
AloeUp Sunscreens at 25 SPF or better are my favorite.
Sun Precautions, 800-882-7860, make a cottony, soft, featherweight fabric called Solumbra that is reported to block out 97 percent of the sun's harmful rays. The shirts and pants are light and loose and quite comfortable.

Nature study books, kits, toys, and games:
Animal Town, 800-445-8642
Educational Insights, 800-933-3277
Klutz Press, 650-857-0888
Wild Planet Toys, 415-247-6570

APPENDIX VI

Maps and Guides

HERE IS A LIST OF RESOURCES TO HELP YOU FIND ACCURATE maps and up-to-date information.

United States Geologic Survey (USGS), 800-USA-MAPS: This federal agency produces topographic maps covering almost all of the United States.

United States Forest Service, Public Affairs Office, 202-205-1760: The Forest Service will send you printouts of facts pertaining to policies and camping locations on request. Ask for *A Guide to Your National Forest,* a large map that details all of the facilities operated by the Forest Service.

National Park Service (NPS), 202-208-4747, 202-619-7222: Request copies of *The National Parks Camping Guide, The National Parks Index, The National Parks Lesser Known Areas,* and *The National Park System Map and Guide.*

Bureau of Land Management, Public Affairs Office, 202-452-5125: Maps of all the BLM lands.

United States Fish and Wildlife Services, 202-343-4311: Although there are very few camping opportunities at Fish And Wildlife-managed wildlife preserves, there are a great number of other recreational possibilities. Many of the preserves provide for boating, bicycling, hiking, hunting, and fishing. Request the map, *National Wildlife Refuges: A Visitor's Guide.*

United States Army Corps of Engineers, 202-761-1534: The Army Corps of Engineers provides a tremendous number of recreational areas open to camping on a first-come, first-served basis. Many of these areas also offer boating opportunities. Request maps of all the sites by writing the main office, or request specific site information by writing each district office managing that area.

Canada Map Office, 613-952-7000: A source of topographic maps for all of Canada and the Northwest Territories.

Trails Illustrated, 800-962-1643: A source of waterproof and (in my opinion) the most up-to-date topographic maps of our nation's national parks, as well as many recreation and wilderness areas.

Tom Harrison Cartography, 415-456-7940: Produces excellent topographic maps of parks and wilderness areas in California.

Earthwalk Press, 701-442-0503: Publishes topographic maps for Western parks wilderness areas and recreational areas in Hawaii.

Appalachian Trail Conference, 304-535-6331: Topographic maps of the Appalachian Trail as it winds its way through the 14 states.

Wilderness Press, 510-843-8080: Publishes topographic maps that coincide with the company's excellent field guides for the Sierra and other areas in California.

DeLorme Mapping, 207-865-4171: DeLorme publishes topographic atlases for most of the 50 states. An excellent resource for planning purposes.

Wildflower Productions, 415-558-8700: Excellent CD-ROM maps for Yosemite, the San Francisco area, and others.

APPENDIX VII

Dealing with Insects

INSECTS HAVE INHABITED THE EARTH FOR MORE THAN 350 million years. They seem to act as if they own the place. It appears at times that Homo sapiens was placed on this planet as food for the little biting nasties. Since the first human hand swatted vainly at swarms of mosquitoes, man has been trying to repel an insect onslaught every time he heads outdoors.

Mosquitoes, fleas, ticks, and black flies all have bites that cause painful irritations at best and debilitating or fatal diseases at worst. Repellents, when used properly, can prevent bites and transmitted infection.

Besides dressing in light-colored clothing that protects as much of the skin surface as possible, you have to decide which repellent is best and safest for your particular needs. What I've tried to do below is answer the questions I am asked most often so that you can make the best choices.

Q. What is Deet?

A. You're not likely to find the word Deet on any repellent label. That's because Deet stands for diethyl-toluamide. If the label contains this scientific name, the repellent contains Deet. Despite fears of Deet-associated health risks, and the increased attention given natural alternatives, Deet-based repellents are still acknowledged to be the best protection against insect bites.

Q. What are the health risks associated with Deet?

A. A number of deaths and a number of medical problems have been attributed in the press to Deet in recent years. The makers of Deet vehemently deny that these problems were specifically related to Deet, and point to reams of scientific documentation as evidence. It does seem logical to assume that if Deet can peel paint, melt nylon, destroy plastic, wreck wood finishes, and damage fishing line, then it must be hell on the skin—perhaps worse.

Although nothing definitive has been published, there is a belief among a growing number in the scientific community that repeated applications of products containing low-percentage levels of Deet can be potentially dangerous. The theory is that this actually puts consumers at a greater risk for absorbing high levels of Deet into the body than if they had just used one application of a 30- to 50-percent Deet product with an efficacy of four to six hours. Also being studied is the possibility that low levels of Deet, which might not otherwise be of toxicological concern, may become hazardous if they are combined with solvents or diluents (considered inactive ingredients) that may enhance the absorption rate.

Q. Are natural alternatives a safer choice?

A. To imply that essential oils are completely safe because they are "natural" products is not altogether accurate. Essential oils, while derived from plants that grow naturally, are chemicals too. Some are potentially hazardous if ingested and most are downright painful if they find their way into the eyes (common with children's wandering fingers) or onto mucus membranes.

For example, pennyroyal is perhaps the most toxic of the essential oils used to repel insects, and can be deadly if taken internally. Other oils used include citronella (perhaps the most common, it is extracted from an aromatic grass indigenous to southern Asia), eucalyptus, cedarwood, and peppermint.

Three citronella-based products, Buzz Away, manufactured by Quantum; Skin-So-Soft by Avon; and Natralpel, manufactured by

Tender, have received EPA registration and approval for sale as repellents for use in controlling mosquitoes, flies, gnats, and midges.

Q. How effective are natural repellents against ticks?

A. Manufacturers are not supposed to advertise that their products repel ticks, according to the EPA, because data regarding citronella's effectiveness against ticks is inconclusive. The same applies to the effectiveness of other natural chemicals against the persistent tick.

Q. What does an EPA registration mean?

A. EPA registration demonstrates the product to be safe for human use according to minimum EPA guidelines. Remember, any product claiming insect repellence on the label must obtain EPA registration. In addition, any biochemical product using essential oils as an active ingredient greater than 2.5 percent must also obtain registration with the EPA. The industry generally regards as ineffective any formulation using less than a 10-percent mix of citronella.

Q. How effective are natural repellents?

A. While there are numerous studies cited by those on the Deet and citronella sides of the fence, the average efficacy (effective repelling time) of a citronella product appears to range from one-and-a-half to two hours. Tests conducted at Cambridge University, England, in 1993 comparing Natrapel to Deet-based Skintastic (a low-percentage Deet product) found citronella to be just as effective in repelling mosquitoes. The key here is efficacy and the amount of time to reapplication.

Citronella products work for up to two hours and then requires reapplication (the same holds true for other natural formulations). Products using a low-percentage level of Deet also require reapplication every two hours to remain effective. So, if you or your child are going outside for only a short period in an environment where insect bites are more an irritant than a hazard, you would do just as well to use the natural product.

Q. What other chemical alternatives are there?

A. Another line of defense against insects is the chemical permethrin. What makes permethrin so good is that the human risks are dramatically minimized, since the chemical is applied directly to the outer fibers of gear or apparel. Permethrin chemically binds to the fibers, which minimizes inward migration and possible skin contact. Permethrin-based products are designed to repel and kill arthropods or crawling insects, making them a preferred repellent for ticks.

Q. How long does the spray-on version of permethrin last?

A. The currently available civilian products will remain effective, repelling and killing mosquitoes, ticks, and chiggers, for two weeks and through two launderings.

Q. Can Deet-based or natural products also be applied to fabrics?

A. While it's true that you can use Deet on clothing, its application is limited to natural fibers. Deet will quickly melt synthetic fibers, and it's most embarrassing to watch your pants melt right off your body.

As far as long-term application goes, naturals do not lend themselves well to either skin or fabrics. Industry officials report that trials are being performed with a certain herbal repellent as a fabric treatment, so there may in fact be a place for fabric treatment with natural repellents in the near future.

Q. What do the experts recommend to prevent tick bites when adventuring in tick country?

A. Wear long pants that are tucked into the socks as well as long-sleeved shirts tucked securely into the pants and held with a belt. Clothing should be light in color making it easier to spot ticks, and tightly woven so ticks have trouble hanging on. You must perform tick checks regularly. It is best to have a buddy check you, and, no, this is not a good time to be modest.

A combination of Deet insect repellents applied to the skin and permethrin repellents applied directly to clothing, tents, sleeping bags, and any surface other than skin are considered to be the most effective line of defense against ticks.

Q. Are there child-safe insect repellents?

A. It is generally acknowledged that children should not use insect repellents with a high percentage of Deet—the lower the better, with 10 percent being the recommended dosage. Most companies offer lower-percentage Deet-based products. Pump sprays or lotions are often the easiest means of application. Deet-based products using synergists or other methods, in addition to reduced percentage concentrations, are considered the safest alternative by many.

Although they are not as effective as Deet in repelling insects, natural-based insect repellents offer an alternative to parents seeking potentially less chemically toxic means for preventing bites.

Q. Do repellents work against bees, wasps, and other stinging insects?

A. No. You can, however, avoid attracting undue attention by following a few simple guidelines. For a start, dress in light-colored clothing. Studies have shown that black, red, and blue are more attractive because bees and their other stinging cousins see in ultraviolet. Do not wear perfume or cologne because the sweet smell seems to attract insects of all kinds. When you are planning a picnic, keep in mind that fruit, red meat, sodas, and food packed in heavy syrup are like dinner signals for hornets, yellow jackets, bees, and wasps.

Should a stinging insect make frequent fly-bys through your personal space, resist the urge to wave wildly and swat blindly. Instead, use (and encourage your children to use) a gentle pushing or brushing motion to deter the incursion. Wasps, bees, hornets, and yellow jackets don't react kindly to quick movements.

Q. What should I do if I'm stung?

A. Cool the sting area with a cold compress. If you were stung by a bee, scrape the stinger out with the edge of a knife (don't cut yourself) or your fingernail. A product called the Sawyer Extractor works very nicely here. It uses suction to remove the bee venom and stinger. Do not attempt to grab the stinger and pull it out as you will only inject more venom into your skin by compressing the venom sack. If the pain persists, add a topical ointment such as benzocaine to the site to numb it.

INDEX